v

WELSH COUNTRY ESSAYS

WILLIAM CONDRY

First Impression—May 1996

ISBN 1 85902 395 9

Printed by Gomer Press, Llandysul, Ceredigion

CONTENTS

PREFACE

Though not a native of Wales, I came here early. I was still in the infants' class at my school in the Midlands when I was brought to Wales on holiday and I thought it was Paradise. So the country caught me young and when I grew up I lost no time in coming to live here. Subconsciously perhaps that holiday delight I got when five years old has never left me. One day at school in my teens I had to write an essay on: 'What did you do in the summer holidays?' And when I think back over all I have written about Wales in the last half-century, I suspect that I may have been writing that school-day essay all this time.

Many of the pieces in this book have appeared over the years in *Country Life*. Others, though written long ago, have not been published before. I have not attempted to update any, in the hope that the passage of time may have burnished some of them with a touch of historical interest. They are in chronological order and are dated as accurately as I can remember. I offer them as a record of countless enjoyable experiences and wonderful places in this fair land of Wales.

BIRMINGHAM'S RIVER

One day last June I took a bus-ride from Aberystwyth and got off at Pontrhydfendigaid, a village which lies to the west of those Welsh moorlands from which Birmingham gets its water supply. I heaved my rucksack onto my back, crossed the humpy bridge over the River Teifi, turned left up a lane and headed for the hills. I had long known this region to be perfect exploring country and on that lovely summer day I wanted to find the source of the Claerwen River and follow it down to where it flows into Birmingham's newest Welsh reservoir.

For a mile my road ran straight and level along the valley. Chaffinches shouted along the hedges, curlews yodelled from the meadows and buzzards were wailing high in the blue sky. I soon reached the ruins of the Abbey of Strata Florida and from there I struck left across the Teifi, slanted up through hillside oakwoods and came out onto a hill-top where larks were singing all round. Now I could see the higher moors ahead of me like a barrier. Soon I left the last trees behind and then the cottages in the valley passed out of sight. The way grew rocky and steep. But at last I topped a ridge which gave me a wide view of treeless hills peeping over each other's shoulders far away into the distance, with here and there the silvery glint of a lake. I had reached the watershed. Behind me the streams all hastened west down rocky valleys and wooded glens to Cardigan Bay. But in front the water of every lake, marsh and stream of this plateau would be making its way towards England.

It is often difficult to decide just which is the source of a river and so it was with the Claerwen. I finally traced it to a wide stretch of marshy ground where a spring of crystal water came welling up among cushions of brilliant green moss and overflowed into a network of runnels in the heather-covered peat. For a long way the water is slow-moving on the almost flat top of the watershed; but where it feels the ground beginning to slope, it makes up its mind, gathers its threads into a tiny brook that winds between tufts of purple moor-grass and very soon it receives its first tributary that comes trickling down from a lake. From there, its volume increased, it becomes a gurgling, musical rill clearly committed to an easterly course to find the Wye. Or, what Birmingham wants of it, will go to the great pipe.

A rambler with a rucksack on his back does not move as smoothly down with the Claerwen as water flows. Instead I found myself stumbling over tussocks of grass and onto softer and softer ground until water was over my boots and I had to go a long way round to avoid sinking right in. A kite circled above me as I reached a moorland pool called Llyn y Figyn ('Bog Pool'), which was almost hidden in its own tall vegetation, a place for waterfowl and marsh birds. Here I accidentally flushed a teal off her eggs deep in the rushes. Two or three pairs of these little ducks were evidently breeding there and were reluctant to leave the water as I approached.

A red kite circling over the source of the Claerwen

Bog rosemary, an uncommon plant with pale-pink flowers, grows on the peat moors where the Claerwen rises.

When they did get up, I was, as always, struck by how neatly they sprang into the air and how exciting was their racing flight, their green wings flashing in the sun as they turned. From high in the sky came that strangest of sounds, the bleating of a snipe, so lovely to hear in the silence of the hills.

Crossing from Cardiganshire into Radnorshire, I made my way round to where the stream slips smoothly out of the lake in a deep channel it has cut between walls of black peat. Here I was delighted to find that rather rare little plant, the bog rosemary. Then I went down a cleft in the hillside, a cleft which broadened as I descended. This was the beginning of the Claerwen valley which I could now see curving away below me towards the south-east. Before I went down I took a last look at that great treeless landscape of long, level ridges that stretched north into Montgomeryshire, south to the Brecon Beacons and east to the heights of Radnor Forest. Then I went down into the valley of the Claerwen.

Everything now I thought would be plain sailing down to the reservoir which was hidden round a bend in the valley. But after I had followed the Claerwen for another two miles, it passed under a little stone bridge, for here a track from over the moor crossed the valley and disappeared away to the north-east. I wondered greatly at that lonely track making its way with such singleness of purpose into the wilderness. I examined it. It was a grit and stone road on which much labour had been spent, though at what period of history I could not guess. Certainly it had the look of age and its original purpose had clearly long ceased, for it was almost ruinous. I was not surprised to see that my ordnance map marked it as an Ancient Trackway.

Seeing this I wavered. Roads marked as ancient are almost irresistible to the mountain walker, especially a track which, according to the map, went on and on across the moors, passing the northern tip of Birmingham's Elan reservoirs and then heading across the Wye. It was almost certainly a medieval road linking Strata Florida Abbey with the Abbey at Cwm-hir twenty miles away. I knew that another branch of this old road was one of the drovers' roads along which until a century ago cattle used to be driven in great herds on the first stage of the long trek from west Wales to the Birmingham market, so that Midlanders could get their beef fresh. Either of these branches would have been fascinating to follow over the moor. But now it was late afternoon so I thought it best to leave the old roads for another day and continue my way down the Claerwen.

The stream now wriggled from side to side of a bare, flat-bottomed valley enclosed by steep slopes several hundred feet high. The going became easy over sheep-nibbled, springing turf and in a short time I saw ahead of me where the stream suddenly broadened round a curve of the hill. I had reached the head of the Claerwen Reservoir and in a few minutes this great sheet of water stretched before me, dark-blue and wave-flecked between its green hills. I knelt and drank from my cupped hands and thought of the millions of thirsts this water would slake at the other end of the pipe.

For four miles I followed the curving hillside above this new lake until I looked down from the high dam into the lower Claerwen Valley. Now I was on a metalled road for the first time since I had left Pontrhydfendigaid fifteen long miles back. Trees began to appear as I went down towards Rhayader and soon slopes were leafy on both sides with oakwoods and there were farms and cattle and men working in the fields: the first people I had seen since early morning. I found they had little Welsh and spoke English with almost a border accent. So already, in the very centre of Wales, I had left the Welsh language behind; for though the place-names are Welsh enough nearly the whole of Radnorshire speaks only English, as is inevitable in a land cut off from the rest of Wales by mountains and which has always looked towards England for its markets.

Certainly the village of Elan looks as English as you would expect since it was built by Birmingham Corporation. It looks like a mature and pleasant suburb, a bit of Moseley or Edgbaston that strayed into Wales fifty years or so ago and has settled down very comfortably there in the leafy valley overhung by the great dams that stand one above the other up the Elan Valley.

At Elan the pipe begins. It slips down the last few miles of the Elan Valley, tunnels under the railway and over the Wye below Rhayader. Then up the other side, curving round a hill with the main road; but when the road begins to bear too far south the pipe sheers gently directly east.

Then it slews round to leave Radnor Forest on the south, creeps over into the Teme valley at Knighton, edges north to avoid Bringewood Chase and so to Ludlow. Then across Worcestershire by gentle undulations to Cleobury Mortimer; straight down through the Wyre Forest; over the Severn between Bewdley and Arley; over the Stour north of Kidderminster; a climbing curve to get round the Clent Hills, down through Hunnington and so to Frankley Reservoir; and after 70 miles the water is out of the pipe at last.

But the highest ground round Birmingham is all on the west and south-west: from Oldbury through the Clent Hills and Frankley round to the Lickey Hills. This means that the natural drainage of the city is towards the north-east. So that when the Welsh water has dropped from the heights of Bartley Green Reservoir into the city and has fed the factories, cooled the towers, washed the cars, watered the gardens, bathed the bodies, flushed the toilets and satisfied the thirst of well over a million people, it still finds itself pressing on eastwards, then northwards and eventually into the Trent. By the time it gets to the Humber it has crossed both Wales and England and is 200 miles from its source. In fact it has followed a course far longer than the Severn which is reckoned Britain's longest river. So if anyone asks you what river Birmingham stands on, do not say the Rea, or the Tame, or the Cole, or Hockley Brook, say it stands on the River Claerwen which rises in the uplands of Cardiganshire and flows into the North Sea at Hull and is by fifty miles the longest, though perhaps not the wildest, river in Great Britain.

(1952)

11

A FLASH OF RED

House-sparrows are not so inevitable about human dwellings as many people think. I have lived in three cottages in different parts of the Welsh hills and never seen a sparrow under their eaves. But there were redstarts at all three, nesting in the walls or not many yards off, and you cannot have redstarts about your cottage all day, singing on your chimney or chasing each other across the garden, without getting very fond of these loveliest of summer birds.

If the songs of willow warbler and tree pipit are eagerly listened for as a sign of spring's return to the hills, very welcome too is the bright flash of red tail-feathers along a wall which is often one's first glimpse of a redstart. What unwonted colours the first cock redstart brings to the still sombre April woods! Black cheeks and throat, white forehead, light-grey crown and back, reddish breast and fiery rump and tail: this sudden bright vision reminds us how starved of vivid colours are our northern eyes most of the year. By the end of April redstarts are abundant in their Welsh breeding haunts; and the nature of these haunts surprised me when I first came to Wales from the English Midlands. For there, in the district where redstarts were most plentiful, I knew them as birds of dry, sandy parkland, scattered with pine and birch, and their nests were usually in holes in trees well away from humanity. But here in Wales they are frequently upland birds, haunting hanging woods, sheep-farm buildings, field-walls and the walls of cottages whether inhabited or not: they seem to prefer to nest in artificial sites and are often close neighbours of man.

Their special haunts here are the wooded slopes along mountain streams: cool, wet places green with ferns and mossy rocks, where the male bird's song is hard to hear in the noise of white-splashing water. Yet even there, where they seem remotest from man and where the gnarled and rotten trees offer many a good hole, the redstarts prefer to lodge their nests in a man-made site: a boundary wall, a mill-ruin, a lead-mine relic, the shell of a slate-shed. If none of these is available they will use the woods for feeding and roosting, but nest in a wall some distance away.

To me there is a strange quality of wildness in the redstart's song, in that brief tremulous opening phrase. What follows varies much from bird to bird: it may be a rattle or a hoarse squeak, but sometimes a long plaintive phrase of indefinable beauty. Of all spring's delights one of the greatest is to hear the dawn song of several cock redstarts singing loud and close to each other in the hillside oaks. Listen on a mid-May morning from the hour when the dawn-light touches the higher slopes. Above the trees a nightjar reels his last song, tawny owls cease their hooting, the first wheatear scratches out a few notes from among the dark rocks. Then, quite suddenly, inside the wood, redstarts and robins come one after another into song and for perhaps thirty minutes have the still morning to themselves. The quick, vehemently repeated phrases of the redstarts and the slower, richer music of the robins come more purely to the ear at that hour than at any other.

Boldness and shyness are curiously merged in the redstart. We have had pairs build in our cottage walls, a few yards from the door, with people constantly about. This suggests that they are inclined to be familiar, like robins; but they are not. They nested in our wall because the hole there was a deep, dark one not to be improved upon in their area and because they had used it in previous years when the cottage was empty. So, despite our presence, not because of it, they used it again, overcoming their fear of us. But they remained shy, silent and evasive as long as they could. The hen came to the nest always from round the back, slipping so quickly into the hole that we were not even sure she had built until one day we looked and found six blue eggs in the nest. The cock, too, kept away, and usually sang from a hedge a hundred yards off. Only when we were very quiet indoors would he venture into the garden to sing from the apple-tree close to our window. His song at four yards' range was lovely to wake to in the morning. One day—the first morning he arrived—he perched on the open window and looked into the bedroom, no doubt wondering if this 'cave' had any possible nesting-sites in its recesses. I am sure that redstarts, like pied flycatchers, could be attracted more about houses in the hill country by the provision of nesting-boxes, for they will use them fairly readily. One pair I heard of built in the tool-box of a hay-elevator which had been left out all winter. Another pair nested in a pile of wood-shavings on a carpenter's bench.

It was with some astonishment that our farmer neighbour, passing by one day on his round of the sheep, beheld at the end of our cottage a crude platform on tall poles on which we were erecting a square tent of sackcloth for the observation and photography of the redstarts. For now the eggs had hatched and both parents had changed their demeanour abruptly. Now they became bold, indifferent to intrusion: their alarmed *poo-it chic-chic* became a constant sound above the cottage. Then it was a joy to see them landing together on the grey roof-slates, beaks full of flies and caterpillars, their orange tails atremble, and a few seconds later disappearing with a final splash of red into the hole in the masonry. We could compare them then as they waited on the low roof, eyeing us anxiously. Perhaps, after all, the hen, in her quiet plumage, is the lovelier of the two: her large eye showed more lustrous against her light feathers, her soft-grey wings went beautifully with the bright orange tail. But the cock, unlike many cock birds when feeding young, was much the bolder. He would fly out in front of our faces, cross to the hedge, quickly grab together a beakful of green or brown grubs and return straight past us into the hole. Only the presence of the timid hen made him also hesitant. She went no farther than he for food, making a speciality of grasshoppers caught on the bank behind the cottage.

Throughout the last day that the young were in the nest the cock called as if with deep anxiety. But I do not think this really betokened anxiety. It was, like the incessant *wee-tac* of whinchats at the same season, an unconscious development of voice which at the appropriate hour serves to call off the young. Meanwhile he still sang often, though now almost solely the vibrant opening phrase. The young seemed to leave the nest rather prematurely, for, instead of flying away, they fluttered down to the wood-pile, where they remained all day and roosted. Next day they were strong enough to go and the cock now used a new note to call them off, a husky *chat-chat* which the young repeated exactly. So off they went to the hawthorn thicket, five of them, light-spotted, dark-brown little creatures, young robins except for their bright tails. We saw them about for a few days and then no more. None of our redstarts have had second broods.

(1954)

FLYCATCHER OF THE WESTERN WOODS

In the 1950s the future was looking bleak for the pied flycatchers of parts of Wales as so many broad-leaved woods, beautiful but uneconomic, were being clear-felled to make way for conifers. But that destructive phase came to an end and now we are all conservationists. In recent decades large numbers of nest-boxes have been provided in some of the woods and no bird has responded more eagerly than the pied flycatcher. It has not only increased in Wales but has even spread in good numbers beyond Offa's Dyke. So today there are many woodlands in western England where you can go in spring and hear the delicate songs of pied flycatchers where they were seldom heard before.

A pair of pied flycatchers at a nest-box on our bedroom window-ledge.

The ancient and beautiful hillside oakwoods of Wales, whether they clothe the lower flanks of the mountains, or cling along the plunging sides of narrow valleys, or hang over gorges, these woods of sessile oak have a character and a fauna which set them apart from all other present-day British woodlands. For these damp, undergrowth-free, often rocky, always wind-swept woods are the haunt of three rare creatures: polecat, pine-marten and kite. To the botanist they offer not so many flowering plants as more primitive forms of vegetation: lichens, liverworts, mosses and ferns in delightful profusion. To the bird-watcher they offer in spring not the full chorus of bird-song audible in a lowland wood where undergrowth is abundant, but the songs of lesser singers not commonly to be heard together elsewhere: the delicate songs of wood warbler, redstart and pied flycatcher.

The cock pied flycatcher, with his two or three sweetly repeated notes, is almost inseparable from these western valleys. At the flowering season of the wood-sorrel and the golden saxifrage, he belongs more than any other bird to the world of straight, thin oaks tiered steeply above one another on the mossy wet slopes.

Occasionally pairs will nest away from woods in scattered roadside trees, or even on the outskirts of villages, or in lowland gardens. But ninety-five out of a hundred in Wales nest in oakwoods, often where their songs come indistinctly through the noise of streams in rocky places.

The period of full song is short. The cock of one late-arriving pair had been singing for 10 days only when his song began to dwindle, about May 26, with the laying of eggs. But, if brief, the song is persistent. A very tame cock, which last year adopted a nest-box on our bedroom window-sill, sang his few notes with endless repetition from dawn till evening a few feet from our windows, especially during the two or three days before the hen arrived and while she was building. In most parts of these woods pied flycatchers are common enough to stimulate each other into rival song, and often three or four at a time are within hearing.

An April or early May cock pied flycatcher makes full use of his conspicuous black-and-white plumage to call attention to himself. His incessant song is often uttered from an obvious bare twig, high up for all to see. At human intrusion he will frequently fly down and sing or scold from a few feet away. He is the most aggressive small bird I know. Right from the first hour of his arrival in a territory already long occupied by resident birds, he starts a programme of deliberate and persistent assertion. From a strategic perch he swoops like a shrike, not nearly so much on passing insects as upon other birds. Robin, chaffinch, hedge sparrow, all are driven off with a flurry of pied wings, the pursuit being brief and ended suddenly.

It is the hole-nesters, however, which he recognises as his special rivals; tits and nuthatches which are his favourite victims. Standing intent on his high twig, his tail slowly working up and down (it has a thin white line down each side for an added touch of display), he dashes down wildly on one bird after another, routing several in a few seconds. Or he has a strange way of more gently parachuting upon them like a courting blue tit or a flight-singing wood warbler. In either event his intention is clear: it is not physical attack, but assertion through display, for the whole affair goes with much tail-spreading and wing-fanning. The two white spots on his forehead add to his ferocious look. He is a true cousin of the butcher-bird.

His plumage is deceptive: he is often neither truly black nor truly white. Close to, the black lacks depth and often appears brown, especially on the spread wing. Catching sunlight, his back will appear ruddy-brown, as does a willow tit's cap. But individuals vary much from one to another. Sometimes the primaries are quite brown in any light, and in some birds even the tail-feathers, the most consistently black feature, appear dark brown in bright light. The breast is not really white, but silver-grey and silky in texture.

After aggressiveness, curiosity is the male's outstanding attribute. Without any visible hint of hostility, he will follow a prospecting nuthatch in and out of hole after hole, tree after tree. This nuthatch-pied flycatcher association occurs every spring in woods where both species are common, lasting for just those few unsettled days after the flycatchers' arrival. Cock pied flycatchers will sometimes follow enquiringly after people, visit their gardens, and most readily adopt their nesting-boxes. But mainly their inquisitiveness is directed towards the activities of other birds. I watched one cock pied flycatcher standing quietly twelve inches from a chaffinch and listening to its singing for nearly half an hour without moving. When the chaffinch flew, the flycatcher followed close behind. Another came and perched on a mid-stream stone to watch a blue tit bathing. Another divided his attention about equally between myself and a pair of coal tits I was watching at their nest.

To describe the hen pied flycatcher, after the male, is like turning to another species. Bird photographers like the male's contrasting plumage, but there are in the hen subtle beauties and delicate markings which make her an even more attractive, because more challenging, subject. Her ways match her looks. Where the male is bold and assertive, she is shy and easily missed. Now and then she will drive away other birds, but I have not found her at all inquisitive. At first sight, especially on the wing, she is rather warbler-like, grey-brown of back, silvery-breasted. But see one working along a hedge with a willow warbler, and the comparative stolidness of the pied flycatcher becomes apparent. A warbler restlessly weaves through the twigs, stretching sharply and slimly forward for insects, or fluttering delicately after flies.

A pied flycatcher will also search for caterpillars, but more often waits, dives out,

A hen pied flycatcher taking a characteristic cautionary peep before leaving her nest.

(Harold Wright)

snapping its bill loudly, and then carries on to another perch, rarely returning like a spotted flycatcher. Standing still, the female has often the look of a hen chaffinch. She does all the nest-building, mainly using coarse dry grass, quite long pieces, and a few dead leaves, all gathered within a few yards, if possible. The cock occasionally takes in a grass, but only as a formal gesture of courtship. Mainly he sings in front of the hole, sometimes following her into the nest with an excited sizzling note, and coming out again immediately and waiting for her. In most of the nests I have seen there have been six or seven eggs, rarely eight, very rarely nine.

Intrude upon pied flycatchers when the young are growing up, and both parents will fly from perch to perch close around you, calling out their mild alarm note, a single, half-suppressed *pwit*. The cock, being less directly concerned with the nest itself and more intent upon the keeping of a territory, is often more excited than the hen by human intrusion, but less ready than her to visit the nest. As soon as the spotted, robin-like young are on the wing the whole family immediately disappears, presumably to follow an unobtrusive wandering life high in the leafy tree-tops of full summer. One week a valley may seem full of pied flycatchers. Next week we find none at all.

(1954)

THE SURPRISING SPARROWHAWK

A sudden smashing sound, a tinkling of broken glass and a pigeon-sized bird lying stunned on the window-sill: such has been more than one countryman's introduction to the sparrowhawk, for hawks have not the understanding of the peculiar properties of glass which many small garden birds have. On such an occasion it would be well to look closely at this bird while we have the chance, for in a few minutes it will be up and away. Note the slim bullet-shape for speed; the long heavy tail for sharp cornering; the wings strong for power yet rather short for slipping neatly between trunks and through branches; the eyes which look forwards and yet which look sideways and backwards also; the very sharp down-curved beak for meat-tearing; above all look at the thin but steel-strong yellow legs and feet taloned for killing. Now the hawk recovers consciousness. Its eyes open. One of them is bruised and blood-filled and will take time to heal. The other is large, round, yellow, black-pupilled and has that fixed staring quality peculiar to the eyes of birds of prey. Take up the hawk—you'll be surprised how light it is—go outside with it and let it feel the breeze. One moment it will be dazed and limp in your palm and in the next it will have burst out of your hands and flown round the nearest corner almost too quickly to see.

In those few minutes you will have seen a side of the sparrowhawk's character which places the bird apart from all others, even from other British birds of prey. For in pursuit of prey sparrowhawks are the embodiment of intentness, tautness of nerve and recklessness. With perfect singleness of purpose they select an individual from a flock of small scattering birds and follow headlong its every twist and turn until either they catch it, or it drops into cover, or until some man-made obstacle to which hawks are not by nature adapted to avoid—a window, a green-house or a wire-netting fence—brings disaster.

The tense, nervous sparrowhawk, so unpredictable. What other bird of prey could suddenly sweep round the corner of your house, perch on your gate and stare at you in your garden at a range of six feet? Yet this has happened at our cottage, which is adjacent to a wood beloved of hawks. How few we notice even where they are common, so careful are they when not hunting to keep out of man's way, to fly on the other side of the hedge or to keep below a bank. How often these silent birds must slip close behind our backs unnoticed, or even pass unseen before our eyes, so dark are they and so low do they fly along the dark ground. In the woods we would seldom know of their presence were it not for that peculiar shrill chorus which

A female sparrowhawk. The male hawks seldom come to the nest.

(Harold Wright)

17

tits set up—especially long-tailed tits—whenever a sparrowhawk flies close. In more open country the hawks become more obvious. Where I live in mid-Wales nearly every wooded valley has its several pairs and they, hunting singly, frequently pass up the dingles of tributary streams, cross the bare shoulders of the lower mountains in quest of small moorland birds and glide down another dingle back to their valley. Or they leave the valleys for far skirmishes across the lowland fields; or over the fresh marshes to the estuaries where they hunt not the open mudflats but rather along the lines of embankments and gutters; or they follow the shoreline to veer suddenly up over the cliffs or skim aside through sand-dunes: going everywhere at the same steady high speed with rapidly beating wings or stiff-winged glides usually only a few feet above ground. They do not sight their prey from afar like a peregrine, or from overhead like a kestrel. They rely entirely on surprise, confusing their prey by the unexpectedness of their arrival. If they strike and miss then they have lost the advantage of surprise and often make no second attempt. The usual prey of a male sparrowhawk is birds of finch or thrush size but the bigger female kills many woodpigeons and magpies in the woods, and on the shore takes waders up to at least the size of oystercatchers. Locally sparrowhawks seem to specialise in hunting for a particular species: one I observed seemed to kill nothing but great tits; another, chaffinches; a third decimated a jay population.

If one's usual view of a sparrowhawk is dissatisfyingly short there are occasions when their flight can be observed at length—when they are soaring. I have seen this every month from November to April but mostly in late March and early April. On calm, fine days particularly, the male, sometimes the female, and occasionally both, will circle on outstretched wings and widely fanned tail, the primaries slightly parted at the tips, over the nesting wood or an adjacent hill, sometimes spiralling up till you need a field-glass to see them. These courtship flights are worth watching throughout for they may end with an exciting steep plunge by both birds together down into the trees below.

Though so faithful to the oakwoods of the Welsh valleys it is remarkable how infrequently the sparrowhawks actually build their nest in an oak. The sessile oaks, growing close together, are but thinly leaved and then only at the crown. The hawks prefer thicker cover and if there is a dense old spruce growing amid the oaks there they are most likely to build. Failing that the hawks like nothing better than a plantation of tall larches for nesting in. But though they like cover I do not remember seeing a nest in an ivied tree. Occasionally their nests are but slight and precarious: one I saw was in a thin holly and so badly supported that it tipped day by day at an ever steeper angle until the eggs rolled out into the gorge below. I have heard of sparrowhawks breeding on cliff-ledges in north Wales but the nearest I have seen to such a site was a nest four feet from the ground in a dwarfed, windswept larchwood high on a steep Montgomeryshire hillside.

At the nest the female sparrowhawk is almost the opposite of wary. What infinite precautions we took, in building our first hide by a hawk's nest, to add a fragment at a time at intervals of several days. And what a surprise we eventually got when we found that this bird, so difficult to approach in the field, was boldness itself at the nest, a boldness quite ludicrous when, wanting the hawk to change to a position more suitable for photography we found, after making experimental low sounds, that no matter how much we increased the noise the hawk stayed rigid at the nest. My strangest experience with a wild bird is that of sitting in a tree-top hide shouting my loudest at a hawk ten feet away and getting no reaction beyond an inquisitive cocking of the head. But shake the canvas wall of the hide ever so slightly and she is gone like a bullet. A spell of watching at a sparrowhawk's nest is a wonderful experience. If the young are still small and downy it is not long before the female returns to the nest. There will be a short spell of calling close by—a shrill *ki ki ki ki ki*, lower pitched than the kestrel's similar note, followed by dead silence as the bird listens. Then a thin whistle of wing and with startling suddenness there is the big hen at the nest. Her white breast is well barred; her back is a dark reddish-brown which in certain lights look slaty. She has a pale line over her eye. (This is a bold streak in some hens, lightly pencilled in others.) It is hard to persuade oneself that her staring eye is not looking right through the hide. She holds a plucked, unidentifiable bird firmly in her talons and from this she energetically tears morsels with her bill and distributes them to her twittering, excited young ones, eating the bones and the bigger pieces herself. She walks round the nest and then settles on her young to brood them, though until they quieten down she is tossed about like a ship on a rough sea. The nest is kept clean right to the end, food not being allowed to accumulate on the nest as it is with buzzards and kites. The male hawk is usually as timid as his mate is bold. At most nests his visits are very rare; and if he comes at all he is likely to drop his prey into the nest in flight and vanish immediately, which is why good still photographs of male sparrowhawks are scarce. Male sparrowhawks vary a lot: while all are blue-grey on their backs, some have whitish, some bright-pink breasts. A bird of the latter type is such a brilliant creature with the sun lighting up his colours that I have always wanted to see more of him at the nest than I have. The male announces his arrival with food by a repeated, buzzard-like *kee-o kee-o* uttered from a nearby tree and then, normally, the hen goes to him for it. The food-cry of the young hawks, after they are past the twittering stage, is a cat-like mewing which is the nearest they can get to the adults' buzzard-call and which they will keep up in chorus while being fed and even afterwards. The result is a volume of sound audible downwind for a quarter-mile, a dangerous advertisement of the nest site.

Some of my happiest bird-watching memories are of hours spent in hides by the nests of hawks, harriers and buzzards. Only then can you observe these vigilant birds off their guard for long periods and get to know something of their personalities and the way they react to the trivial events that make up their daily lives through the months of the breeding season. In April there is the care which the female sparrowhawk puts into selecting and assembling just the right thin sticks for the nest and just the right bits of bark for the lining; in May and June the thirty-three or so days of motionless sitting on the eggs, oblivious of the flies constantly walking over her plumage, as indifferent to small birds feeding in the branches about her as they are to her; and after midsummer the weeks of caring for the young in the nest. A hen sparrowhawk occupied with the little incidents of nest-life is a delightful subject. One I watched used to stare for long periods at her young after feeding them, occasionally picking up a stick in her beak and with deliberation carrying it round to the far side of the nest only to return it to its former position a little later. Another accidentally dropped her prey from the nest. She listened carefully as it fell through the twigs to the ground, walked to the nest-edge and looked down for some moments and then fluttered down like a dove to recover it. Perhaps what I have learnt chiefly from my long watching of sparrowhawks is how much more there is to their character than the bent for killing; in short, how unhawk-like they are most of the time.

(1955)

BLACKCOCK AT DAWN

I could not write about blackcock today as I did in this account of 1956. The young conifer plantations are now tall timber trees unattractive to blackcock. Perhaps when the trees are clear-felled and the site re-planted the blackcock cycle will begin again.

Blackcocks nested among these young conifers but came out onto the open ground to perform their courtship rituals.

Out into the dewy dawn this April morning to see the display of the blackcock. Years ago this would have involved a long and perhaps fruitless journey into remote mountain country, but today, with forestry plantations spreading everywhere, the blackcock has become easily accessible, for no bird is more intimately linked with coniferous forestry. So now I have only to go a mile from home up onto the nearest hills to hear the strange bubbling of the blackcock any time of the day, but especially morning and evening.

The last owls called as I walked through the deep wet tussocks of purple moor-grass up to the rocks I had chosen as a watching place. It was getting dimly light and the wind was cold. Quietly I settled in the shadows with my back against a rock and waited. Though I have heard the blackcock a great many times the first musical bubbling that breaks the silence of dawn is still as good a sound to me as if I heard it for the first time. It is a wild and primitive call that takes you right out of the twentieth or any other century, straight back to the earliest dawns of life. The rocky outcrop that hid me was just outside the forest fence, commanding a view of a grassy arena that sloped down to the trees. Presently I heard the first blackcock calling. A long silence. Then he came flying from the shadowy trees into the half-light outside the fence. There he stood and bubbled and gobbled and curtseyed and displayed to nothing more responsive than a sheep. But in a few minutes a second blackcock appeared from somewhere, soon followed by two others and immediately the whole play was on. What a strange performance it is, all these stylised dawn rituals, these leapings into the air, these struttings and cavortings, these bowings and tail-raisings, these displays of scarlet wattles and of white tail-feathers against black ones. We can sit at home and see close-up films of it all on television and hear the wonderful noises that go with it. And both vision and sound may well be clearer than we can experience in the field. But it does not live as it lives in the greyness of the dawn.

(1956)

ARAN FAWDDWY'S RIVER

Lately I have followed the River Dyfi upstream from its mouth in Cardigan Bay to where, 2,500 feet above the sea, it flows out of the grey rocks of Aran Fawddwy. Measured on the map its valley is about thirty miles long but the river itself is twice that if you allow for all its wriggles.

To anyone with a mind to explore this little river I would recommend a boat for the first part of the journey, though I admit it will not get you very far on your way. Preferably go in the lightest canoe or coracle you can lay your hands on. Certainly nothing keeled; nor, worst of all, engined. For these first few miles will be above all an experience of the silent movement of the tide as it goes inland; something to be awaited for a whole month or even two, till you get that extra big spring tide that some calm morning will carry your canoe to the furthest possible point upriver.

At first, taken at its flood, the tide will almost race you up the estuary along creeks winding between sand-banks till after four miles it funnels you into a narrowing channel and sweeps you round the bend under Glandyfi Castle. In the silent company of a fleet of driftwood, straw and flotsam, you pass between broken-edged saltings loud with singing redshanks. No need for navigation except to keep amidstream and avoid the pillars of the railway bridge just ahead. Here for the last time the river is deep, murky, voiceless and estuarine. Here on the stanchions of the bridge you will find the last seaweeds upriver. (They are Montgomeryshire seaweeds,

View north across the Dyfi estuary at Glandyfi to the hills of Meirionnydd.

Bridges over the Dyfi at Dinas Mawddwy. The higher bridge carries the present main road. The lower one dates from earlier centuries.

incidentally, for that essentially inland county that marches with Shropshire extends an unexpected finger westwards to dip it in the brine just here under this bridge.) And somewhere above here, if only we could find it, perhaps not far under the silt, lies in all probability the paved causeway of a Roman ford. For the Roman camp at Pennal, now lost under a farmhouse and fields, stood here on the Dyfi's north bank and here there must have been a vital river crossing linking north and south Wales.

Not that the morning tide will leave you much time for historical musings. For once you are above the railway bridge the world changes quickly. Already the estuary feel has gone. Abruptly you have lost the open skies and far views across saltings: life has narrowed and you are gliding between high clay banks. So you go on your silent way with the sea far behind and forgotten but the sea water still pushing you

inland. But as you go on you become aware that the banks are sliding past more slowly. There is no longer the same urgency in the water. Then at last it takes you listlessly round the final curve and your boat is still. But not for long. In a matter of minutes the tide has turned and you have to paddle to stop yourself drifting seawards. So here you tie up, take to the bank and make your way upstream to Machynlleth.

For the next few miles the Dyfi comes snaking down through its pebble-washes along a wide, flat-bottomed valley. This is the stretch most beloved of sandpipers, grey wagtails, dippers and fishermen, and is the one most familiar to travellers: for here the river goes along with main road and railway until the train goes straight on towards England and the river-valley makes a northward sweep that turns your face towards that stronger, more mountainous country where George Borrow, in 1854, rejoiced to discover that not a word of English was spoken by anybody. You are now getting near to Dinas Mawddwy where for a few miles this part of the Dyfi was followed by the old coach-road that went from London to Caernarfon by way of Worcester, Hereford and Dolgellau. You can still see the picturesque bridges of that long-superseded road below the level of the present-day bridges. Dinas Mawddwy itself, though but a small village, is yet a great name in these parts because people hereabouts still half-remember its importance in byegone centuries when it was one of the independent lordships of Wales. This word *dinas*, remember, means a city. Above Dinas Mawddwy the valley narrows. You lose the main road westwards and follow a lane north with the Dyfi. Now you feel yourself among the hamlets and people of an older world. You feel that in the white farmhouses that look across to each other from the hillsides the old Celtic ways will endure a long while yet.

At last you reach a place where lane and river part company and you must turn west with the Dyfi up a track that climbs away along a bare hillside. For now it is goodbye to trees and fields and farms as you head upwards towards the uninhabited hills where rivers are born. Well above your eye-level a high natural wall of rock blocks the valley from side to side. It suggests a dam and a lake beyond and I daresay there was such a lake in remote past times. But the Dyfi has channelled a way through the rocks long since and now, instead of making a waterfall over this barrier, it comes through it, deep in a narrow gorge, splashing into clear green pools it has smoothed out of the grey rock. The country is now wild moorland rising steeply to mountains on both sides of the now almost

The source-lake of the River Dyfi under the crags of Aran Fawddwy.

23

leapable river. Ravens, kestrels and buzzards nest along the crags that hang above the valley. And high up the side-streams that cascade down through the heather you will hear the strange, repeated note of the ring ouzel. If you are a plant-seeker there is sufficient limestone in some of these rocks and screes to give you such endearing species as mountain sorrel, green spleenwort and even that elegant, rarish little grass, the mountain melick. And there is the occasional delight of coming on wet ledges yellow with globe flowers and Welsh poppies.

Soon the riverside track dies altogether and your feet are squelching among great tussocks of the purple moor-grass which cover the last two ascending miles. Best here to admit defeat and abandon the bog for high ground, keeping the river well below you while you skip along the easy, sheep-nibbled turf of the slopes. As you go, the craggy ramparts of Aran Fawddwy build up before you until, quite suddenly at about two thousand feet, you top a rise and find the shining waters of a lake below you; a deep-looking, bare-margined, oval pool a quarter-mile across, from which the river escapes through a gap at the south-east corner. Deep bare lakes lying in the mountain silence under shadowed precipices have an atmosphere that still speaks to the primitive in us; and when you see this lake of the Dyfi's rising you are not surprised to hear of strange legends that have been invented round it in past times: that here gods and giants have done battle when their heads were turned by lake-maidens of surpassing loveliness. Poking into what the old writers have said about this lake, I find Lewis, a topographer of the 1830s, describing it as a pool containing an 'abundance of lizards' which is clearly an error for newts. The mistake is understandable: the Welsh for lizard is *madfall* and for newt is *madfall y dŵr* ('water-lizard'). On a summer's day you can still scoop out little brown palmate newts from the lake-edge to enjoy the surprise of their bright-golden bellies when you turn them over.

From the cold, east-facing buttresses of Aran Fawddwy, you can look back down the way you have come, beyond the shining lake where the pine-marten may still come to drink, to where the Dyfi goes winding away under the hills. And you can rejoice that this little river still runs wild, free and full of life all the way down to where it meets the salt of Cardigan Bay.

(1956)

A Country Diary

Guardian
24.1.98

MACHYNLLETH: A few days ago I drove nervously across the swollen Dyfi River on Machynlleth's ancient stone bridge. I turned left and made my way to the coast at Tywyn which preserves in its parish church a long narrow stone on which is inscribed the oldest written specimen of the Welsh language, said to date back to the seventh century, its meaning regrettably obscure. It is called, probably without justification, the stone of Cadfan, a holy man who, a century earlier, so the delightful story goes, set sail from Tywyn and landed on Bardsey Island 30 miles away. There he founded a monastery whose fame was to make Bardsey a sacred place for many centuries. And there he dies, perhaps the first of the 20,000 saints who, according to tradition, were to be buried on the island in what, for all I know, really were the good old days. I looked out for Bardsey from Tywyn but islands have a tricky way of appearing and vanishing without notice and there was no sign of Bardsey that day. Along the shore there were plenty of birds, mostly gulls and waders, and I was pleased to see several eider ducks which are very local on the coast of Wales but have long been visiting the Tywyn area, so long in fact that birdwatchers have predicted for years that eiders would soon begin breeding there and so create a new record for Wales. Alas, Tywyn is not to have that distinction because, as I have just read in the current number of Welsh Birds, eiders were discovered last summer breeding in Anglesey and possibly Caernarfonshire too. This is but one of countless valuable items of information in an excellent journal whose current number also includes a very thorough Welsh Bird RE port for 1996. Welsh Birds is available for £4.50 (including pp) from its editor, Michael Shrubb, Hillcrest, Llanwrtyd Wells, Powys LD5 4TL.

WILLIAM CONDRY

CORMORANTS' INLAND CITADEL

To get to Bird Rock (Craig y Deryn) near Tywyn, in Merioneth, could not be easier. You can go by bus if you want. You get out under the Rock, the bus roars off and quickly vanishes round the narrow lane that skirts a knee of the Rock, and you are left in a quiet, green, flat-bottomed valley with mountains and woods all round, an opening seawards to the west and the billowing outlines of Cader Idris to the east. You look up at the face above you, and there, crossing and recrossing the sky, so high and so dwarfed by their surroundings they look like jackdaws, are the cormorants. If it is a still day your ear will catch the gruntings and growlings with which the birds greet one another as they land on the ledges. But they are very far above you and the viewpoint is not a satisfying one.

It is the hill-walker who enjoys the best approach, across country from the south. You climb up through woods, and wind round undulating brackeny hills where wheatears play hide and seek among the screes and the air is sweet with lark song. At last you top a rise and there, dramatically, is the sudden deep rift of the Dysynni valley. And there too, if the wind is right, you first catch the smell. You may still be 200 yards from the brink of the precipice, but if the wind is north a reek comes to you that for a moment bewilders. Smells are linked wonderfully closely in our memories with places, and this one gives you an instantaneous flash-back to sea-cliffs and the beat of the ocean below and the voices of seabird colonies. Then you return to the present, to the lichen-scabbed rocks, the moor-grass blowing in the wind, the encircling Merioneth mountains, the pastoral vale. But though the sea-image fades, the unmistakable smell of seabirds persists.

You clamber cautiously across a scree to the edge, go on to your hands and knees when you feel the wind tear up at you, and peer over. And there a few feet below on the white-washed

A cormorant's nest on Craig y Deryn, 1958.
(Richard Bower)

ledges, their nests almost touching, are groups of sitting cormorants. As your head appears, they writhe their snake-like necks as they appraise you from various angles. Farther along the cliff other cormorants which have not yet spotted you hold themselves upright and unmoving, like great black models of birds stood along the ledges. One holds his wings half open; another stands on one leg, balanced on a big webbed foot. Your gaze travels down the face past a lower group of cormorants, past a crowd of jackdaws fluttering in and out of a fissure, past cliff-foot slopes pink with campion, down to a bright-green field an eighth of a mile below, a field scattered with pairs of white blobs in two sizes: each pair a ewe and a lamb.

Such, then, is these cormorants' unusual view of the world. They look down onto no tossing ocean, but a pattern of fields and farms set among woods and sheepwalks. They have no shoreline to descend to for seaweed for their nests; instead, they flutter up to the slopes above and waddle about the grass, gathering gorse-sticks, rushes and grass. There is no welcoming sea for the young to flop into at the end of their maiden flights. In fact, not a drop of water is visible from their ledges except the thin waving ribbon of the Dysynni stream glinting over its shallows on the far side of the valley. Only the shine of the sea, six miles away, reminds them of their true home. There they must travel for food unless they prefer to fish the estuary or go up to the mountain lakes.

The intrusion of your silhouette onto their rocky skyline is only a short-lived shock for the birds. If you keep still or are gentle about your movements, they soon forget you and return to their cormorantine ruminations or whatever goes on in their minds as they sit there day and night

About thirty pairs of cormorants nest annually on Craig y Deryn.

awaiting the emergence of skinny young from the three or four chalky eggs. Soon their mates arrive, swinging into the cliff on half-closed wings, their primaries almost screaming with vibration. They alight amid a deep-voiced chorus something like 'errug, errug, errug', primal sounds in keeping with birds that powerfully evoke the primitive and suggest the pterodactyl. Then there is silence. The incubating ones become restful again. One of the newcomers retches and vomits a fish on to the nest edge, but nobody wants it yet. Another hangs his wide wings and turns into the wind. For a long while there is no movement whatsoever. These silent, still creatures grouped on their ledge might be a tableau in a museum depicting life groping from the reptiles towards the birds.

Then a wave of feeling travels through the colony. There is talking in high tones, falsetto croaks of contentment which rise to a crescendo of tremulous exclamations. And one after another the birds not on nest-duty dive outwards. The north wind, squarely hitting the face of the rock, sheers upwards, taking each bird with it. On long, shapely wings they ride the updraught together, and circle and play, dive and climb; and two go spiralling up and up and up till they are specks against the clouds. Nothing reptilian about them now. Their uprising is majestic, inspiring. Their descent is spectacular. They come down in a breathtaking corkscrew plunge and roar past to their ledge with a sound as if all their feathers were tearing. In a few moments, the ritual of greeting over, they are still and silent in their places, emotion forgotten. The hours pass, threaded with the same oscillating rhythm of peace and boisterousness. As the sun curves away into the north-west it begins to shine on to the nesting ledges, illuminating one bird after another in a golden light. And now you see the cormorants in their true colours: not black as they looked before, but brown and purple, green and blue. Now you not only see their white faces and thigh-patches, but notice also that some still retain on their heads a few filament-like white

26

plumes they developed in late winter. Only the smell is the same.

This is only a small colony as cormorant communities go, a mere 25 or 30 pairs. But it is historic; though how historic does not seem ever to have received the attention of serious researchers. That it goes back at least a few centuries is a matter of common agreement. But how one would like to be able to distil the truth out of the welter of conflicting local opinion concerning the cormorants' history over the last 60 or 70 years! For while some say there are as many in the colony as ever, others are quite emphatic about an enormous decrease and can recall that in their childhood days 'thousands of cormorants nested on both faces of the Rock'; that is not only on the north but also on the much less precipitous west side. I expect that, as usual in such conflicts of opinion, the truth lies somewhere between, that there never were thousands, but that there was at some recent time a decrease. If so, what date more likely than about a century ago, until which time there was an important herring and mackerel fishery on this coast? If these fish decreased, might not the cormorants also have diminished as a result?

(1957)

A distant view of Craig y Deryn (Bird Rock) in the Dysynni valley near Tywyn.

27

ISLAND OF THE BLEST

Peninsulas are like mountains: they lead you on. Once half-way you must get out to the end. And that is what you feel when you are as far down the Llŷn Peninsula as Pwllheli, in that wrist of lowland that cuts through the mountains to the north coast at Nefyn. There you begin to sense the strong shape of this muscular forearm that jabs south-west into the Atlantic. Now it is but a dozen miles to the end. With every mile the land gets barer, trees and hedges diminishing all the way west into the windswept half-clenched fist whose thumb thrusts south beyond Abersoch to hook round the bay called Porth Neigwl (Hell's Mouth). West of Porth Neigwl truncated fingers push bluntly into the waves: and that is almost the end of Llŷn and the last of north Wales, but not quite. For beyond the fist, beyond two miles of water, a Precambrian finger-tip lies parted from the rest, a five-hundred-foot high rock heaving itself out of the sea as smooth as a rolling dolphin. This is Ynys Enlli which the Vikings named Bardsey.

Seen from the end of the peninsula it might be a desert island, for the brackeny, mountainous back it turns upon the world conceals all sign of habitation. All the same, if you go there do not fancy yourself as a pioneering island-explorer. For whether you are saint or sinner, the number of your kind to have crossed that way before you is certainly legion.

You cannot just skim over to Bardsey in a granite trough or on a green sod as the saints of old used to cruise around on their pious occasions. Mortals of less than saintly stature have always had to find a boat at Aberdaron, and still do. For the pilgrims and holy men of centuries there have been those final exhilarating miles of narrowing roads and widening skies as the last windy headlands, changing with every bend and rise of the way, have taken their final shape. Wherever they came from—and many a local fragment of Ancient Trackway or Pilgrims'

Way lettered archaically on the map of Wales seems to point Bardseywards—all their paths converged here at Aberdaron. All descended the last hill to this last village, which until the motoring age remained an almost unknown huddle of fishermen's cottages round an ancient sea-edge church.

The holiday-makers have Aberdaron now, but you have only to turn from the two or three hotels and tea-shops to the changeless curve of the shore, the surviving old low cottages and the salt-sprayed gravestones, to get a strong sense of the past, of the near-tragic life of fisherfolk struggling against poverty and the sea. A century ago a traveller described Aberdaron as 'a miserably poor village'. Today it looks prosperous, but it is still clustered small enough in its little valley along the Daron not to have lost the village charm. They have not yet modernised the humpy bridge or tidied up the alexanders that adorn odd corners in May with their yellow umbels. Let us pray that enough saintly magic still holds in these fingers of Celtic land to forbid the road-straighteners and verge-sprayers for generations yet.

Though you are going to the island in a motor-boat you have to respect the six-knot tides of Bardsey Sound. Tides do not change and the waves that try to claw out the dead through Aberdaron's churchyard walls are the same as those that have given pause to Bardsey pilgrims all through time. There is still scrambling into an open boat and poling through the breakers to calmer water before setting of sail or starting of engine. Then away to the open sea and an empty horizon; for not until you clear the bay and begin to feel the Atlantic under you do you see Bardsey quickly race into view round the point. Soon you are across and Bardsey's razorbills and guillemots are whirring down at you from the cliffs and skimming just past the boat, and kittiwakes are showering daintily off their ledges and clangouring round you with voices surprisingly deep for small gulls. Then you are gliding between narrow rocks into the only landing cove, leaping ashore in the ancient way and gathering your possessions on to the beach before you follow the road, the only road, the pilgrims' road.

This narrow, rough road lifts you gently to the north end and the unimposing abbey ruins. And there is the end of fact and the beginning of surmise. What was it like, this edifice of which now only a broken tooth of a tower remains for wagtails and little owls to nest in? Who knows what foundations may stretch underground from this old lopped stump, creeping like roots under the farmhouse and buildings against which it is huddled; under the modern burial ground, under the surrounding fields, deeper altogether than the level of present life? But somehow neither the site nor the feel of the place suggests that a great building ever stood here. The feeling is of what the very conjectural history of the place suggests: a modesty and asceticism in keeping with this unwealthy island. In this spirit was the abbey founded, probably by sixth-century monks led over from Brittany by St. Cadfan. And in this spirit it seems to have continued, islanded in piety and unworldliness. So great grew its fame for these qualities that it became the desire of many to end their days on Bardsey in pious devotion, or failing that, to be carried over there for burial. Hence the twenty thousand buried saints poetically ascribed to the place.

But the ages roll, and piety and hermitry had their day even on Bardsey. The end of it all came suddenly. The Atlantic never threw up wave or storm like the Protestant tempest of the 1530s. Along with monasteries and centres of pilgrimage everywhere, Bardsey abbey, its tower, its bells and its parchment rolls were smitten and left to the slow dissolution of time. So a life vanished. Only a few stones, and the abundance of that herb-tea nettle, the pellitory of the wall, often associated with old monastic sites, are left to suggest that monks ever inhabited the place.

After that crofters took over, but crofters who

Bardsey abbey ruins and one of the farms in 1957.

were more fishers than farmers, for Bardsey is a place for people with more sea-longing than land-longing. Their one-storey cottages dotted the island until three-quarters of a century ago, when the present tall houses, solid but alien-looking, were built in their stead. But already Bardsey was beset by the fate of modern islands: the people were drifting away, thinking to improve their lot elsewhere. In 1840 there were a hundred permanent residents, in 1870 ninety, in the 1930s thirty-five, now scarcely half a dozen. As people have dispersed, birds and seals have moved closer in. Grey seals, once persecuted and scarce, now play in the shallows off Bardsey's one beach and watch you with unending curiosity. The sea birds are no longer robbed of their eggs. And, typical contribution of our generation, there is a bird observatory where you can stay and watch migration in progress.

If you can, go to Bardsey in May when the turf is patched blue with squills. Let the path zig-zag you up into the wind across a mountainside yellow with gorse. Stand on the top by what is possibly a prehistoric mound where wheatears scold by day and shearwaters burrow by night. Look landwards across the white-flecked tide-race streaming off the north end and along noble headlands to the shadowy tumult of the Merioneth mountains. Or seawards to where you may see the horizon thicken into the jagged shape of the Wicklow mountains seventy miles away. Or look straight down the plunging slopes of rock and bracken and wiry grass to pink sheets of thrift where shags stand sentinel above their nests, and choughs and jackdaws pry for food.

Or look back over the island spread out behind. Over its little fields and farmyards; across the narrow neck to the bare south end crowned by its boldly red and white lighthouse tower. A green sea is breaking all round the rocks in a curtain of spray filled with sunlight. If those who lived on Bardsey in the days of prehistory could return now, would they see much change in the island apart from the few buildings and the altered shape of the fields? I do not think they would. The essentials cannot have altered: the solid feel of ancient rock underfoot; the sound of water on the shore; the kiss of the wind always fresh from the sea; the weather-signs in the western sky. Small islands like this belong less to man than to the elements, and Bardsey is as Bardsey always was.

(1957)

A NEW BIRD FOR EUROPE

The keen students of bird migration who, spring and autumn, man Britain's bird observatories are a race of optimists who hope for everlasting anticyclones centred north of Europe so that the resultant light easterly winds will divert hordes of Continental migrants west across the North Sea to Britain. And since September is the month with the greatest likelihood of anticyclonic days, which then average more than ten, that is the time when ornithological hopes run highest. All the same, September can also produce deep depressions over the North Atlantic, and these bring high winds and rains raging across Britain from the west to confound all hope of birds being blown here from the Continent. So it was in the second week of September, 1957: there were days of very strong winds which increased until by the 11th high seas were pounding the whole western side of Britain. It was on that day that a strange bird arrived on Bardsey Island off the north Wales coast—a bird so unusual that none of the experts at the island's observatory could at first name it or say what family it belonged to, even after it had been caught and could be examined in the hand.

The first who saw it flying along a hedge said it was like a big greenfinch, but was as yellow as a golden oriole. This was not a bad field description, but in the hand the bird resembled neither greenfinch nor oriole, nor any bird that could be found in the *Field-guide to the Birds of Britain and Europe*. So resort was had to the *Field-guide to the Birds of the Eastern United States*, and it was among the admirable colour-plates of that work that a likeness of Bardsey's strange visitor was found. The bird was evidently a summer tanager, one of an American family of fruit and insect eaters related to the finches. Tanagers, though not found in any other Continent, are represented in tropical America by some 200 species, of which only four migrate

During its fortnight's stay on Bardsey the tanager spent most of its time along a hedge of fruiting brambles.

from the tropics in spring to breed in the United States. One of these is the summer tanager.

We can imagine flocks of small birds, including various tanagers, passing down the eastern seaboard of the United States. As a vast depression deepens south of Iceland an eastbound gale begins to whip across the Atlantic. The birds are whisked out to sea like leaves. Perhaps many perish, some struggle back to land and one, a summer tanager, is hurtled tail to wind over 3,000 miles to the coast of Wales. Supposing it flies at 30 m.p.h., before a wind of 40 m.p.h., giving a total speed of 70 m.p.h., about 45 hours would be needed for the crossing.

We might ask whether a small land bird could fly for 45 hours without rest or food. It seems unreasonable to suppose this impossible. But in any case there are ships to rest on, though not for long because hunger would soon impel the bird on. It is known that migrant birds habitually lose much weight on long sea crossings. That this tanager increased its weight by half while on Bardsey shows how starved it was when it reached the island.

The male summer tanager is rosy red in spring, turning yellow in autumn, and the female is greenish yellow. As the Bardsey bird was yellow, but with flecks of red in two places, it was evidently a male in a transitional stage of plumage. Catching the sun from a hedge-top, he looked a bright all-over yellow. But this was the result of colour suffusion because at very close range only the upper breast and the sides of the neck were a clear yellow; the head was yellow-brown, the back greenish and the wings and tail brown. The heavy, sharp bill was a striking feature, and in it the tanager could hold and chew a big blackberry with ease. And chew is just the word for what the bird did. Of many blackberries I saw him pick he never swallowed one. Slowly he masticated the fruit, swallowed the juice by visible throat movements and rejected the pith and seeds, taking up to five minutes to deal with each berry. The result was that under his favourite feeding perches small piles of chewed blackberries accumulated. Only once did I see him take any other food; this was when he flew deftly out of the hedge to take a passing insect in the air.

Standing alertly, he looked rather like a flycatcher or a shrike, and once or twice, listening to a noise which slightly alarmed him, he erected well-developed crest feathers all over his head and half-cocked his tail. His flight was rapid and direct, reminiscent of redwings dashing out of the winter hedges. Normally he flew low along bank and hedge and when disturbed preferred to fly into the nearest cover rather than go high and put distance between himself and danger. It was interesting to see how this stranger immediately took up a beat or territory for his stay on the island. Though Bardsey has many bramble hedges, the tanager selected a favourite one and spent most of his time there, returning to it despite being often disturbed.

Getting photographs of the tanager after he had been on the island a week and was daily getting livelier and more wary took a long time. For detail I wanted to picture the bird in the hand and that meant catching him, which took several hours. For a natural portrait I wanted the bird in the field and that meant building a hide by a likely perch and waiting for him to come at his leisure. So I sat a couple of hours on the slope of Bardsey mountain observing the tanager feeding along the hedge below and noted the places where he most commonly perched to masticate his berries. Of these favoured perches I chose two: a stick of dead bramble poking out of a bush and a strand of barbed wire across a gap in the hedge. Opposite these points a friend and I built a crude hide of gorse, crude but effective, for a few mornings later the tanager, though mildly suspicious of these intrusions, did at last settle on both of these perches and so got photographed.

(1957)

A male redstart at one of
our window-ledge boxes.

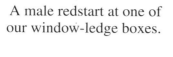

Ynys Enlli (Bardsey
Island).

An immature barred
warbler caught for ringing
on Bardsey.

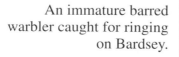

Bardsey
lighthouse
and
mountain.

Hillside
oakwoods
in the upper
Tywi valley.

TO THE LIGHTHOUSE

Since this was written, some of the bird casualties at Bardsey lighthouse have been reduced by illuminating an area of ground nearby. This can sometimes have the effect of diverting birds away from the lighthouse tower against which they might otherwise have crashed.

A soft April dusk and the lightest of airs off the Atlantic. A mist almost drizzle cools our faces as we stand on the top of Bardsey Island's mountain. There will be no stars, no moon tonight. So there will be shearwaters, for it is only on black nights they come to the island. We stand and listen. Behind us, down on the low south end of the island, the lighthouse begins to flash its night-long message out to the Irish Sea shipping lanes. At first there is nothing to be heard except the rustle of the tide moving through the sound, and the capricious slap of water against cliffs five hundred feet below. It is one of those too rare moments of utter tranquillity. We think of wind and ocean and the slow dissolving of rocks through the measureless years. Then an ancient voice speaks, a faint caterwauling high in the blackening sky, and in a few minutes the air is full of primal sounds, wild cooings, sobbings and wailings. The shearwaters have arrived for their nightly courtship play. But as we listen a figure climbs up to us out of the darkness. It is the warden of the island's bird observatory. He thinks that with this mist there might be work for us bird-ringers at the lighthouse.

Half an hour later, by permission of the principal keeper, we stand on the lighthouse balcony that is built out into space round the lantern. A parapet of steel keeps us from the drop below. As the mist thickens into fine rain we wait for the coming of the night birds. We stare into the darkness, listening to the moaning of seals and watching the play of the light's five successive white beams across the island. At first nothing happens. We speak of other lighthouses: of the South Stack at Holyhead our next neighbour north; and beyond it the blinding light of the Skerries which brings safety for ships but death to migrant birds. We think of Skokholm's kindly light to our south, kindly because red, so not alluring to the birds of the night. Then we remember Heligoland as it was in the time of the great German ornithologist, Heinrich Gatke, who died in 1897.

* * *

For over half a century Gatke pioneered lighthouse bird-watching and thrilled the ornithological world with an account of his life's observations that has lost none of its excitement with the passage of sixty years. In *Heligoland as an Ornithological Observatory* bird-migration takes on real grandeur. British bird-observers speak of rushes of birds involving hundreds, sometimes a few thousand. But on Heligoland, thirty miles off the German coast, Gatke witnessed clouds, deluges, cataclysms of birds. Year after year, in spring and autumn, migrants rained upon Heligoland in numbers beyond human calculation. On the night of October 28th, 1882, he saw such a phenomenal passage of the tiny goldcrest that he could only compare it with a snowstorm. Twenty-four years before, he had spent a calm autumn day watching a slow, majestic procession of birds of prey passing over to the south hour after hour. The number of birds Gatke saw was not more remarkable than their variety: by the time he published his records his tally for the island was almost four hundred species. Nor was it only birds he saw from his lighthouse. It attracted moths in prodigious multitudes. He described how in August, 1882, silvery moths, for four nights in succession, passed the lighthouse in millions.

33

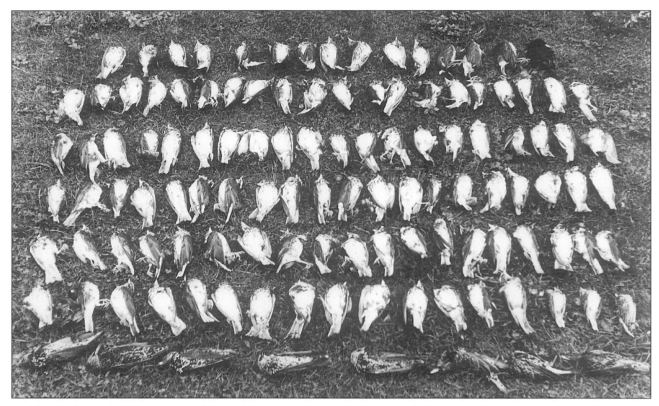

Many birds may be killed in one night by striking against Bardsey lighthouse in bad weather. These were mostly redwings and starlings.

Gatke's work sent others off on the lighthouse trail and it was not long before lighthouse-keepers round the coasts of the British Isles were being asked to report on birds seen or killed at their lights and to send in corpses of unknown birds for identification. The results were revealing. It began to be realised that many more of our common species were migrants or partial migrants than had been dreamt of. The magnitude of the passage of birds up and down the coasts of Britain to and from north Europe came as a surprise to those who had witnessed only visible daytime migration which is usually on a trifling scale in Britain compared with the night movements. Finally, the lighthouse records indicated that many species of birds, formerly reckoned very sporadic or quite absent in Britain, actually pass along our coastlines annually, landing for short rests only on small islands and remote headlands, and therefore escaping detection unless picked up dead at the foot of some lighthouse tower.

Since these lighthouse discoveries the era of the bird-observatory has arrived and now many vantage-points round our coasts are manned by enthusiastic amateur bird-watchers. Their findings have confirmed the work of the lighthouse pioneers and have illuminated it with fresh observations and new ideas. Meanwhile the lighthouses continue to attract hordes of migrants, which is all very well for science but can be hard on the birds which, dazzled by the light, may crash into the tower on nights of poor visibility.

* * *

So we stand on Bardsey tower, all Gatkes for a night. For a whole hour there is nothing visible

34

Two redwings killed at Bardsey lighthouse.

except the endless play of the five white beams sweeping round and spearing away into the darkness. Then we begin to see birds. Or rather we see silver balls come swinging round in the beams to disappear instantly behind us. We catch faint unfamiliar cries, the unknown calls which birds use only on migration. And now a warbler is fluttering at the glass beside us like a moth at a lamp. The warden gently closes his hand over it and puts it into a string-top bag where it will lie quietly for the rest of the night; for once completely dazzled like this a bird may go on beating against the glass till it drops in exhaustion. Next day the bird will be released with an identity ring on its leg. Sometimes the intense glare of the light will upset the delicate emotional balance of these spring migrants. They may burst into song, or spread wings and tail in courtship display, or even play with nesting material.

More and more silvery shapes twirl past, the air is full of whispered cries, and now we are all kept busy taking the fluttering birds from the glass. So the night hours pass; hours of a dream-like experience when we hardly know whether we wake or sleep, a prolonged experience of strange beauty in which we have seen, almost touched, the mysteries of migration and its elemental forces. At last dawn pales in the east, the grey island begins to take shape, and quite suddenly, there are no more birds.

(1957)

LAST LOOK AT HAFOD

Hafod house in its setting in the upper Ystwyth valley, Cardiganshire, just before demolition.

The mansion at Hafod was demolished in August, 1958, shortly after this essay was written.

Hafod, near Devil's Bridge in north Cardiganshire, one of the most famous houses in Wales, looks today so much like a bomb-site that every time I go that way I wonder if it will still be standing on my next visit. Stripped of its lead and the best of its woodwork a few years ago, this empty shell, forlorn memorial of lives and hopes departed, looks ready to totter to its final ruin in the next gale that sweeps up the valley. The moment seems fitting to look back once more on the saga of achievement and woe that was the career of that remarkable man Thomas Johnes.

But first to put Hafod in its place, its quiet,

leafy, mountain-encircled place. Here the little Ystwyth stream, fresh from its moorland sources, comes serpenting down through its pebble-washes under what once were hills clad with woods of Johnes's creating but which today are mostly bare and which tomorrow will be largely conifer-clad: for the property is now the Forestry Commission's. From Hafod the river hastens down the remainder of its dozen miles to the sea at Aberystwyth, beautiful all the way. Yet there is a glint of falsity in its beauty for, like many a shining Welsh stream, the Ystwyth has a long history of lead pollution.

Early leaseholders of Cwmystwyth mine were a branch of the Herbert family who quickly rose to wealth as the mine prospered. Cardiganshire's chronicler, Meyrick, summarises their fortunes with nice simplicity: 'They happened to prosper.

They grew rich and popular. Purchased considerable estates; married into the best families; and kept an hospitable house at Havod for many generations, till the heiress, and last of the name, married to Mr. Johnes of Llanvair and carried with her the estate.' It was a member of this family who in the course of time was to become famous as Thomas Johnes of Hafod who, a contemporary of Sir Walter Scott, grew up with Romantic ideas and applied them in creating this brief paradise up in the hills of Cardiganshire.

Though his first marriage was conventional enough, Johnes astonished everyone, when his first wife died, by marrying a Welsh cousin and going off to live in the wild solitudes of upland Cardiganshire. But it was not to be love in a cottage. He brought with him the Bath architect, Baldwin, cleared away the old house of the Herberts on its flat and leafy terrain above the river, and built in 1783 a light, airy and capacious mansion with pointed arch windows in the Gothic style. Soon Nash, then an almost unknown architect in Carmarthen, was called in to make certain additions. Later Johnes added 'one of the wonders of Wales': the octagonal library in which were housed precious Welsh manuscripts and rare illuminated manuscripts from France. Not that Johnes was a mere bibliomaniac. He was a scholar with a particular enthusiasm for chivalric literature. In his Gothic house, set in romanesque grounds of his own designing, he could lose himself for hours of every day in recreating the age of knights and fair ladies by translating into English the breezy chronicles that Froissart wrote about the heroes of the Hundred Years' War. These translations ('waking old Froissart from his sleep' as Johnes used to say) were a labour born of leisure, opportunity, taste and especially devotion: for into everything he undertook Johnes put his whole ardent self, rising often at four, never later than six each morning to make time for his literary work. Only he and Lord Berners, three centuries before him, have ever put the whole of Froissart's chronicles into English. Johnes's translation was hailed by Scott in the *Edinburgh Review*, and if, though more elegant and faithful, it lacked something of the richness of Lord Berners' translation, it suited his contemporaries well enough. 'You meet it,' said one of them, 'in the stately folio, bulky quarto or portable octavo form in the libraries of almost every well educated Englishman.'

Johnes did not do things by halves. Not content with his writing he had to be his own printer also. So, to the general wonderment, out into the wilds came a printing press which produced the Froissart and others of Johnes's translations. There appeared also his *Landlord's Advice to his Tenants* which introduces another facet of the man. For Johnes the Romantic was also Johnes the agricultural reformer who laboured endlessly to encourage modern farming methods. And if you go to Hafod today almost the only thing left for you to see of Johnes's making, apart from the house, is the monument to Francis, Duke of Bedford, for his services to agriculture.

And there was Johnes the planter of trees. For centuries the lead-smelting furnaces of Cwmystwyth had been devouring the local forests, a process which even 250 years before, Leland had noted as he came down the Ystwyth from Rhayader: 'About the middle of this Wastwith Botom that I rydde yn being as I gesse a iii Miles in length I saw on the right hand a Hille side wher hath been great digging for Leade, the melting whereof hath destroyed the Woddes that sumtime grew blentifulli thereabout'. And now under Johnes's direction the bare slopes were planted with three or four million trees: larch, beech, oak, ash, rowan, birch and alder, some got locally, some from Scotland. All were planted and walled round with care. Details of the numbers and origin of the trees and the methods and dates of planting are to be found in a little manuscript notebook preserved in the National Library of Wales. Although to put beech on these hills was in defiance of precedent, they succeeded. In the course of time they have fallen to the axe so that now but few remain, still thriving monuments to the faith Johnes had when he set their roots in the acid mountain peat 160 years ago.

So Johnes lived and to outward appearances prospered (in reality he was spending far too excessively). He had his beautiful wife Jane, his talented daughter named Maria Anne but always known as Mariamne, a stream of distinguished guests and a battalion of servants and work-people. He saw to the housing of his tenants and provided them with a surgeon and an apothecary. His wife opened a school at Hafod for the free education of poor girls. He himself planned one for boys. Nearly all his energies went into improving people, stock, crops, land. The estate blossomed more each year. Indoors, next to the library, was a great collection of exotic plants. Outdoors there multiplied gardens, walks, waterfalls, grottoes and other curiosities. Twentieth-century taste would scorn Johnes's artifices but they suited his generation. As one admirer wrote: 'Wherever improvement has attempted to add to the simplicity, to tame the wildness, or to prune the luxuriance of the native scenery, she has done so under the direction of just taste and sound judgment'. Sir James Smith, first president of the Linnean Society, came and was enchanted by everything; by the scenery, the estate, the mosses and lichens he found in the woods, and by the youthful Mariamne's spontaneous devotion to botany.

For some years Hafod's halcyon days succeed each other. (No room to recall them here but the whole story was set down very beautifully a few years ago in Elizabeth Inglis-Jones's *Peacocks in Paradise.)* Then comes Friday the thirteenth of March, 1807, the night of the fire. Johnes is away from home. It is a time of intense cold. The pumps are frozen and useless. Flames crackle high and fast through the house towards the precious library. Mrs Johnes, Mariamne and a guest make a hopeless bid to save the priceless old manuscripts. In an hour a mansion and a

centre of learning are consumed and Johnes is poorer by £70,000, for little is insured. Yet, when the news reaches him in London he is undaunted. What mattered as long as his wife and his Mariamne were unhurt? Like the phoenix, he said, a new Hafod must rise from the ashes of the old. So for the second time he built and adorned a house on the Herberts' old site, repeating the grand scale of before, a second riot of stone and mortar, fine furniture, art pieces and library treasures: all this in defiance of black clouds of financial failure climbing up every horizon.

Then, only four years after the fire, came the blow that crippled him: the frail, the beautiful, the talented Mariamne, for whom the wonders of Hafod had been created, died. She was twenty-seven. From then on those who lived carried on as before but from habit now rather than desire. Under the double weight of financial worry and personal grief Johnes survived his adored Mariamne only by five years, five years of failure and agony during which he lived to see first some of the timber—what a wrench that must have been—then the estate itself disposed of.

So ended the Hafod story. It had parallels elsewhere in that age. Johnes's failings were those of his time: a Rousseauan urge to better the lot of the less fortunate, coupled with a want of prudence and practicalness, led others besides him into impulsive speculations and extravagences. Then there was his naive faith that tenants and fellow landlords would follow his example of devotion to the land. After Johnes Hafod passed through several hands and for the rest of the nineteenth-century alterations and additions were many. The First World War took its share of the timber but it was the second that finally devastated Johnes's great woods of beech and oak. Then the demolition agents got the house, leaving the present owners, the Forestry Commission, with the unenviable responsibility of deciding how to dispose of a dangerous ruin with perhaps more sentimental than architectural value. And since the preservation of historical buildings is not part of the Forestry

Commission's duties, the possibility of Hafod Mansion ever being restored seems remote.

Looking down today on these ruins should we see in Johnes's saga nothing but failure, nothing but a wreck of impracticable dreams? It may have seemed like that to Johnes himself in his last sad few months of retirement in Devon. Yet pioneers often seem in their time to have failed and it is not until generations later that their ideas are taken up and find fruition at last. Perhaps Johnes was one of these.

(1958)

The last of Hafod house. The beeches beyond were planted by Thomas Johnes, probably in the 1780s.

SPRING IN THE HIGH WOODS

James Thomson's notion of spring: 'Come, gentle Spring! ethereal mildness, come' is as we all know in our fitful climate only a convention of poets. I suppose it arose because poetry in his day had long been saturated by influences from Greece and Italy, where spring is a more certain season. We know spring as the opposite of gentle; if it is really mild one day, the wind is pretty sure to go round into the north the next and blow really cold. As a Scotsman, Thomson ought to have known better.

But even in Britain there are two sorts of spring: the prolonged, less unkind spring of the plain and the late-arriving, icy-fingered spring of the mountains. The people of the Welsh uplands have an expressive word, *hirlwm,* which means 'long bleakness' and which refers to those endless weeks that drag between midwinter and the time when the grass begins to grow again in mountain pastures.

In some years it is not until June that the oaks come into flower in the highest woods.

Hirlwm is the word that comes to my mind when I think of spring creeping into the high woods that stretch black along the wintry hillsides, and do not even yellow until after the valley woods are deep in leaves. What a glad time that is when you can make a mid-May scramble up through the mossy rocks, up into the oaks, and see the unfurling leaves turning from yellow to palest green, and see the long, thin, male catkins shaking in the breeze. In such a wood you are not confronted with bare trunks merely, but live for a while in close intimacy with high branches, buds and leaves. You have tree-tops all about you, even below you, and chaffinches shouting into your ears. You clamber on to a rock the size of a cottage and can examine the flowering twigs without so much as reaching for them.

They are never great trees, these contorted, crag-grasping oaks of the old rocks of Celtic Britain. No 'wooden walls' ever came from them, only fuel for furnaces, bark for tannin, stakes for fencing. I know that Cowper wrote:

Sage beneath a spreading oak
Sat the Druid, hoary chief

but that was no mountain oak but one of the great pedunculate oaks of the lowlands, the sort that Shakespeare knew in Arden. But it was as a mountain tree that Sir Walter Scott knew the oak:

Aloft, the ash and warrior oak
Cast anchor in the rifted rock.

Yes, that is just how they grow. Many an acorn has sprouted in the heart of a cleft rock and produced an oak that for want of root-hold has had to anchor itself by spreading its trunk across a face of rock to grip its edges as a man does in climbing.

Other trees flourish among the oaks, notably

birch and thorn and ash. Of these the ashes are much the last to leaf, and you can pick them out clearly in the woods in late spring by their still bare, whitish branches sticking out like antlers above the leafing oaks, their thick bold twigs curving against the sky. In summer you can know the ashes from afar by their different green; often a belt of grey-green among the bright-green oaks and lying in a straight line down a woodside from top to bottom. Not planted so by man as you might at first suppose, but because some stream flows or some dampness seeps down the woodside there. For ash loves the damper places provided the moisture is neither excessive nor stagnant; not because it is a great drinker but because it loves the richer soil that gathers along the runnels and streamsides.

Who does not like to feel the smooth hardness of an ash-stick, or to see in winter the stiff silvery twigs with their pairs of black buds and the big, swollen bud at the tip? In the high woods it may be June before these buds throw open their black doors, to release dense purple clusters of primitive, petal-less blossoms that stand so bushy and stiff along the twigs that from a distance the tree seems already in leaf. How quickly they sprout, these flowers of ash, and how soon they fade and fall. Only a few days does the woodpigeon have to find them and gorge on them before they are gone and leaves are sprouting in their stead.

'The ash,' said Virgil, 'is loveliest in woods.' Perhaps he was thinking how pleasant it is, when you have been under the deep shade of other trees, to find when you arrive under an ash how the feathery, mobile leaves filter the sun's light into the woods and chequer the ground with dappled shadows.

And under the trees? In most parts of the high woods you will find flowers neither abundant nor varied. Thin, acid soils are the domain of heather, bilberry and moss. In seeking spring flowers in such woodland you may well let the ash trees be your guide. For they, as I said, find the richest, or least poor, spots in the wood and it is at their feet, in the damper areas, that you will find the flowers: yellow and green mats of golden saxifrage hanging over dripping rocks; violets, wild strawberry, primroses, sanicles, ground ivy and others that riot in the lowland woods but which, up here, have to be sought for plant by plant. Tennyson made a well observed point, perhaps better than he knew, in the line:

by ashen roots the violets blow.

In the same situation he might have chanced upon another plant of humble stature, so humble that its very name, Adoxa, means 'of no account'. This little musky moschatel was long hounded from one family to another by botanists unable to trace her true affinities. Once classed as an ivy, she was for a while promoted to close kinship with honeysuckle, guelder-rose, elder and wayfaring-tree. But now science has despaired of discovering her next-of-kin and has left her all alone, sole member of a unique family. So there is food for thought for you some soft April day when you see the first fragile square stems and pale triple leaflets of moschatel pushing delicately through the litter of last year's oak leaves: by what infinity of chance and change through evolutionary time has this small

Moschatel, best-known in lowland woods and hedgerows, is also found in upland woods and on mountains.

plant come down to us, so bereft of relations? Were they even of less account in the struggle for survival than moschatel herself, and so perished?

How cheering it is to find that this flower of no account is after all something unique in the world. What other plant unfolds, from a yellow pinhead bud, a cube of four green clock-faces with a fifth looking skywards? Then there is the plant's respectable world range. Never think of moschatel, if you know it only in soft southern woods and hedges, as a half-hardy cringer in the shelter of giant neighbours. For if ever you are lucky enough to see the Arctic flora you will find our little moschatel braving it out there on the tundra, springing up in the wake of the melting snow. And in Britain you may find it far up the flanks of our mountains: which brings me back to the high woods, especially those on limy soils where ash is abundant.

There comes to my mind a remote Welsh valley on a perfect day in May. I had followed a stream up through woods of ash and oak, botanising casually and thinking I ought to meet with moschatel in such a rich place. But if it was there it eluded me, and I came clear of the trees at last. I was now faced with a long scree topped by a crag. Here I forgot my plant-hunting at the sight of a tiercel peregrine—patrolling back and forth on a slow gliding beat far above me. The crag looked a promising nesting place, and sure enough as I toiled up the scree the falcon came flickering off a ledge, to chatter with deep, angered notes as she hurled herself about the sky. But as is usual with peregrines, the nest was not to be reached; at the top of the scree I found my way blocked by 20 feet of sheer, slimy rock. So I looked about for plants instead. But it was not until I squatted to eat my lunch that I saw beside me, in the shadow of a boulder where it could never have seen the sun, a small patch of moschatel that looked down a thousand feet onto the woods where I had sought it.

Though spring may come late to the upland woods there is this compensation: that in some May drought in the lowlands, when all the green gaiety of the spring has dried up into brownness and seed, you can go to the wet gullies of the high woods and find the year still new there, and rejoice again in the delicate crimple of opening primrose leaves, and find wood sorrel and windflower still fresh and fragrant in a green, unthirsty world. Then, when oak-rollers and geometers have decimated the foliage of the lowland oaks, and the hot woods are unpleasant with the rain of caterpillar-droppings, you can climb to the hill-woods and find the oak leaves clean and almost untouched. For there in the cool upper air insect life is far less abundant. It is as if the high woods are swept clean by the mountain winds.

(1958)

DUNELAND DELIGHTS

This essay of September, 1958, celebrated the declaration of a National Nature Reserve at Morfa Harlech.

The ordnance map shows us Morfa Harlech whose name stretches in capital letters across the whole flat land overlooked by Harlech Castle. This Welsh word *morfa* is a marriage of two words *mor* (the sea) and *fa* (a place). My dictionaries variously translate it for me as sea-brink, salt-marsh, bog or fen. And as you look across its flat expanse, where only in our day houses have begun to venture, you can easily picture the whole stretch from Harlech to the estuary of the Dwyryd as once being continuous marsh, several square miles of wild saltings, creeks and fens; though I daresay we would have to go a long way back to find a Morfa Harlech that was entirely marshland.

Today a very different Morfa exists. Man has long since laid hands on the place, ditched it, drained what he can of it and bit by bit extended his fields towards the sea. A great haunt (we may suppose) of wild life, of plants, birds and other creatures of marsh and water, has been tamed. Some of it has become pasture land. Some of it has served as a military training ground. And now some of it is being planted by the Forestry Commission. But still a choice and sizeable fragment remains, a bit of the former wilderness that not even busy-fingered twentieth-century man has found fit for his use. This is the salt-marsh and sand-dune area tucked away in the north-west corner furthest from habitations and now a National Nature Reserve. Here naturalists, especially botanists, can be truly happy. Not that they are likely to see anything very rare unless by chance the dune helleborine, which was reputedly discovered a few years back, but which no one has been able to find since. But what these dunes and marshes offer is variety and profusion: so many different stages of dryness

Marsh helleborine, an orchid abundant in damp hollows in the dunes at Morfa Harlech.

and wetness from arid dune-top to deepish water; so many different aspects producing, for instance, a different flora on the south and north sides of the same dune; so many different degrees of acidity or non-acidity from the leached soils of the dunes to the lime-rich hollows of the slacks.

For the flowers at their best go to the *morfa* at full summer, when you can walk in the sunlight through the shining plumes of the downy-oat grass and the common blue butterflies flutter away all about you. On the dunes you will find not an array of large showy plants but low and carpeting sorts, gems you must bend to see: yellow dune-pansies; that tiniest dandelion, the smooth cat's ear; the common and the slender centaury; sea-milkwort; field gentian; stork's bills of every size; a good variety of trefoils; thyme, hound's tongue, sea-holly, blue fleabane, both the dune spurges, burnet rose and a great many more delights. And everywhere the sharp fragrance of sand-dunes. Or if you like more primitive plants there are adder's tongue, moonwort and horse-tails.

It is not in the dunes but in the marshes that colour is extravagantly splashed, in the acres yellow with irises. If there were nothing else on this *morfa* it would be worth a visit to see these irises and the hundreds of black-headed gulls that burst in a white explosion from them as you approach. And among their nests you find other plants: three kinds of aquatic speedwells; red rattle of bush-like stature; common and lesser water-plantain; pale-yellow stars of the square St. John's wort; and pond-weeds, sedges and rushes.

Then there are the orchids. Our wild orchids have a great following of enthusiasts. Some of them are seekers of what is rare among orchids: monkey, military, ghost, lizard and so on. Morfa Harlech is not for them. But if you rejoice in profusions, deluges of orchids no matter how common, if you like those species that nature casts at your feet with uninhibited generosity, then go to Harlech.

First in time come the green-winged orchids of May, mostly red-purple, a few pinks and a few whites: all about six inches high, profusely scattered in the rough of the links, thinning towards the dunes. As they fade, the marsh orchids are beginning and it is these that are this *morfa*'s greatest delight, and also its greatest despair, these seldom straightforward, sometimes unidentifiable marsh orchids.

These we are told may be species in the act of evolving, striving for stability of form; but, insufficiently distinct from one another for the normal rough and tumble of inter-specific rivalry, they end by flowing into one another and the result is a bewildering infinity of hybrid forms. Here the lovely little deep-coloured *purpurella* of the north meets the taller, paler *praetermissa* of the south. Here the parents stand side by side and around them proliferate their intermediate offsprings. This would be fairly simple if it were all. But the *incarnata* orchis can scarcely be ignored at Harlech, for this is the most abundant marsh orchid of the whole place. And it too hybridises with the rest.

Finally, to make confusion further confused, both the heath spotted and the common spotted orchids are here, crossing with the marsh orchids and with each other. It is hardly surprising that often the greater task is to find not the offspring but the original parents of these mixed relationships. Frequently no parents exist, having been crowded out by their descendants long since, for often the intermediate forms tower up with hybrid vigour to reach over two feet in height and carry six or eight inches of glorious purple spike.

But perhaps hybrids are not to your liking. If not, you may turn with relief to the assurance of more solid species. *Orchis incarnata*, for instance, though I mention it as sometimes hybridising, is for the most part pure at Harlech and from the golf-course nearly to the edge of the salt-marsh its brick-red variety, *coccinea*, is in scores in every marsh and dune-slack. With them you will see rosettes of sharp leaves in crowded hundreds and these later on will produce the other orchid wonder of this place: countless spikes of the lovely marsh helleborine. Also there are the twayblades and the deliciously scented butterfly orchids. Then, but in most years uncommonly, you may find on the drier slopes a few bee orchids and rather more pyramidals. Finally, September brings a handful of autumn ladies' tresses.

I have many bird-watching memories of Morfa Harlech; of, for instance, a perfectly still

One of many plant-rich wet hollows in the dunes at Harlech.

evening at midsummer, the only near sound being the hiss of the spring tide making haste across the sands. In the foreground the dunes and dune-grasses are cut out almost in white against the great blue arc of mountains that curves from Llŷn to Hebog and on to Snowdon, Cnicht and Moelwyn, then round to the Rhinogydd close in the east. Overhead is endless lark-song; in the distance are faint exclamations of nesting redshanks and the incessant far-off wailing of the black-headed gullery. I lie watching stock-doves in courtship about their nest-holes in the sand. From another burrow a shelduck waddles forth and, taking wing, flies down the sands to meet the tide. Then a dozen curlews come high across the sky. In silence they head out to the estuary and seem to be about to cross over when, dramatically, the flock explodes and each curlew comes yelping earthwards in a wild power-dive, corkscrewing down like a stricken aeroplane, with a violent sound as of tearing feathers. All land simultaneously on the sands, immediately

fold away great beaks under their back feathers and stand in silence to wait for the tide.

And I remember a mid-winter day. This time I am lying hidden in the marram on a dune-top overlooking the gullery-pool. Now the gulls of summer are dispersed, perhaps wintering far to the south and the pool has other occupants. Brilliant blues, greens and chestnuts flash in the sun off the heads and wings of mallard and teal splashing and scuttering in courtship play. Even more colourful are a group of shovelers feeding half out of the water just below me. A shelduck, a pintail drake, some pochard, a few coots, moorhens, a dabchick . . . there seems hardly room for such a crowd on so small a water. Then, like white yachts appearing round the curve of a river, four wild swans, three whoopers and a Bewick's come swinging round a bend of the dunes, and they too somehow find a place on the pool. I ask myself: could there be any more intense experience of life, movement and colour than this?

(1958)

A SPRUCE LITTLE BIRD

Whatever the rights and wrongs of large-scale afforestation, there is no doubt that the excluding of sheep and other grazers from large areas of moor and mountain and the planting of trees in their stead is an experiment of marvellous interest to the naturalist.

Nature never wastes a chance like this. Not only do grasses and such plants as heather and bilberry rejoice in this release from the dreadful incisors of the flocks and herds, but countless insects, spiders and other small creatures also respond to this ecological revolution. And attracted by them and by the wealth of lush grass and seeds come a multitude of small mammals, followed inevitably by larger, predatory mammals and birds of prey. Meanwhile thousands of little conifers grow up and in their cover breed a host of small bush-loving birds—warblers, finches, hedge sparrows, robins, yellowhammers and so on—species which are normally alien to mountain habitats. Of these small species one of the most interesting and least noticed is the lesser redpoll, a little finch known to be increasing in Wales where it has become one of the most successful colonisers of the upland conifers and now breeds in most forests where trees are at the right stage.

The right stage is vital. When a forest is planted there is an immediate move-in of whinchats and tree pipits. They are nesters in the long grass and enjoy the tiny conifers as perches. In the next few years the trees pass through a gooseberry-bush stage, thickening into one another to form a low, impenetrable jungle. By this time the whinchats and tree pipits have abandoned the site but undergrowth-lovers such as hedge sparrows, bullfinches and warblers have come in. Then up shoot the trees to ten, twelve, fourteen feet. It is at these heights that they are attractive to redpolls.

The best redpoll locality I have known was a moorland valley in Wales which some twenty years before had been planted mainly with Norway and Sitka spruce all over its flat marshy bed at 1,000 feet and up its steep sides to about 1,300 feet above sea level. Here there nested some twelve to fifteen pairs of redpolls. But it is wise to be cautious in estimating redpoll numbers in such a breeding haunt, for the birds seem to be everywhere at once as they fly about high over the trees, constantly crossing the valley from slope to slope, ranging the whole stretch of the forest, exploring the tributary valleys and even wandering up over the rim of the forest on to the open hills above.

Redpolls have no regard for that division of an area into territories which dominates the lives of most other land birds at nesting time. In favourable weather they are never long in advertising themselves by their song-flight, which may be performed by single birds or by several together. They begin by perching in a

A redpoll's nest in a plantation of Sitka spruce.

group, each on the tip of adjacent firs, singing or calling. Then all burst steeply into the air with a hurried chatter of short notes. Rising to about fifty feet and keeping close together, they fly with a quickly undulating, almost hopping flight which in a few minutes may bring them back in a circle above their starting-point, to which they pitch steeply down together. Or they drop to the trees perhaps a hundred yards, perhaps half a mile, away.

The song is simple. It is a rather toneless trill, *trrrrr*, which alternates rapidly with the typical low flight-note which is usually written as *uch-uch-uch-uch*. Both sounds carry far and in spring or summer a male redpoll never seems to fly without uttering one or the other. In full song he has a third characteristic note: a ringing but tinny *tew tew tew tew*. Their liveliness formerly made redpolls extremely popular cage birds, but I cannot think that anyone who has seen their wild free flight over the breeding ground could ever want to see a redpoll, any more than a lark, in a cage. These song-flights begin very early in the morning. Listening to the dawn chorus in mid-May in an upland conifer forest, I found that redpolls began sixth in order of singing (being preceded by whinchat, song-thrush, cuckoo, ring ouzel and willow warbler), but that their song was by far the most sustained over the whole day, though even redpolls have occasional hours of silence. Only on very windy days are they mainly silent, especially if there is cold and rain with the wind.

The nests I have seen in conifer plantations have varied from between two feet six inches to ten feet from the ground. They have nearly all been built against the stem of a tree and resting on two or three fairly level thin branches; but I have seen a few out on flat sprays a foot from the stem. All have been in thickets of unthinned Sitka spruce, not inside the most impenetrable clumps but on the fringe of such where the trees, although growing close enough to touch each other, nevertheless allow you to push your way between them. A few nests have been alongside rides. Some of them have been well hidden, but most of them, placed just above eye level in the more open portion of the tree, have not been so difficult to spot as you might at first fear when you are faced with the prospect of searching through acres of closely planted spruces for the nest of a bird whose behaviour may give you little clue as to the whereabouts of the nest.

Once found the nest is easily identified by the smallness of the inside cup, even though the outside may be fairly bulky. A typical conifer-built nest begins with a loose base of tiny, dead spruce twigs. From that foundation it is built up mainly of dry moss, with an interweaving of hair, bits of dead fern, thin straws, wool, rootlets and similar material as available. The lining may have a feather or two in it or a little wool but is commonly a substantial pad of willow down.

An incubating redpoll is often quite indifferent to near intrusion by human beings. One hen remained upon her eggs while I put up a hide only six feet from her, during which operation I frequently brushed against the nesting tree and tied strings to it to support the hide. When I saw how tame my first redpolls were at the nest I supposed that photographing them would be simplicity itself. It was not so. For even when incubating, when other species are very still and watchful, the hen redpoll cannot rest. She is constantly shuffling, yawning, turning about, nibbling at the rim of the nest or deeply into the nest or turning to look up at passing birds, especially crows and hawks. If another redpoll flies over, the sitting hen will sometimes quiver her wings and call softly. So that delightful as it is to watch these lively little birds you can spoil a lot of film in trying to catch their movements.

Whenever I see this eager colonisation of the conifer forests by all these different creatures I am reminded of the Latin refrain of a song we learnt at school: *Ubi bene ibi patria*. This might be translated by our forestry redpolls as: 'We shall be quite happy to settle in this neck of the woods for ever provided the trees remain just as they are'.

Cwm Einion near Machynlleth. The young spruces in the foreground were the nesting place of a colony of redpolls for a few years in the 1950s.

But alas! the redpoll-stage of conifers does not endure. Where the trees are growing well it may last four or five years only, and then the trunks get tall and slender, the bushiness so dear to most small birds is gone for ever and the forest reaches those strangely silent years of its maturity which W. H. Hudson likened to 'the twilight and still atmosphere of a cathedral interior'. Then though there are more large birds than before almost the only small birds are the needle-voiced goldcrests and the occasionally drifting parties of mixed tits. By then the warblers, finches and redpolls will have gone to seek friendlier shelter in new plantations.

(1958)

View north across the
dunes of Morfa Harlech.

A redpoll at her nest
in a young spruce.

Puffins being observed
on Skomer.

The north face of Cader Idris.

Welsh poppy
on Cader Idris.

UP THE CLYWEDOG

My walk up the Clywedog took place nearly ten years before the valley was drowned by the present reservoir in 1967.

An altogether blue, cloud-sailing, beckoning April morning as I go off to revisit an old haunt—the stretch of country that shelters to the east of Plynlimon. Leaving my car at Llanidloes where two rivers meet, I walk not up the Severn which is the natural and ancient pathway to the west, but up the deep and wooded valley of the Clywedog which, like the Severn, has its source on Plynlimon. Everywhere the delights of the upland spring: shining, green river pools, leafing hazels, sunlight shafting deep and bright into leafless oakwoods, dippers singing on midstream rocks, a glistening white plume of black-headed gulls streaming behind a tractor ploughing down an impossible-looking slope on a far hill.

The valley narrows. Steep, unploughable, rock-broken slopes close in on me. Abruptly the trees become sparse. I come to a long-abandoned lead-mine and watch a hen wheatear carrying straws into its ruined walls. A long-tailed tit steers a huge white feather into a blackthorn. I wade the river and clamber steeply to a lofty hill-fort that looks far down the valley. For a while I try to trace its banks and entrenchments; then I sit and rest and look about me and think of time and eternity, two good themes when you have far views of mountains and valleys, the sun is warm on the grass, a singing woodlark circles above you and you are sitting on man-made banks that are still good banks after two thousand years. How many generations have climbed that hill, wondered about the purpose of those banks and speculated about the meaning and brevity of life?

I return to the river and go on up its narrow V-shaped valley to where it makes a sharp bend. I eat my lunch looking into a deep, clear pool under a rock where a great trout swims tamely round and round. Carefully I flick him bits of food but he spits them all out quicker than he takes them. Wishing him long life (but doubting if so unwary a fish would achieve it) I now leave the Clywedog, for it is edging me too far north. I take to a rough, climbing road that looks as if it ends at the grey stone farmhouse I can see ahead of me. But like many Welsh farm roads, this one winds through a dog-yapping yard between the buildings and the house and goes on its way towards the uplands.

The next hill is crowned with a long, narrow windbreak of storm-battered pines whose tops all curve sharply away from the south-west. Chaffinches sing in the mountain wind, a hare runs from under my feet, a kestrel slips quickly out of a pine and away round the curve of the hill. In the tree-tops are several old crows' nests wonderfully surviving the gales of past winters. Wondering if the kestrel is using one of these old nests I make my way through the trees. But the bird that at last flies out of one of them is no sharp-winged, red slip of a kestrel but a long-winged, grey, blundering moth of a bird that drops clumsily almost to the grass, flies along the ground and rises sharply to perch in the top of a pine thirty yards away. She is a long-eared owl, a rare bird of isolated strips and blocks of conifers in parts of the Welsh uplands.

I follow the line of the trees. The whole billowing length of Plynlimon is now close before me; and below me is the last of the upper Severn valley. How changed all that place is since I first knew it years ago! The hollow below me in those days was a great saucer of wet and rushy moorland which had just been planted with infant conifers. I had walked through the long grass there and by chance a short-eared owl had sprung off her nest at my feet. I still have a vivid memory of her as she rose into the sky, then floated slowly away on long, pale wings, an almost invisible bird against the bleached grass of the hills. Today that whole country is deep in trees. All the landmarks I knew have gone; rocks, roads, even houses, swallowed into a heavy pelage of spruces whose dark horizon now reaches almost to the ridge of Plynlimon.

The short-eared owl breeds very sparingly on the Welsh moors. Here the nest was in a new plantation of Sitka spruces on the eastern slopes of Plynlimon.

ON THE FINGER-TIP OF GOWER

I walked westwards along the sunlit cliffs of Gower. A blue sea flowed to meet shining headlands and swept foaming into the bays between them. Over the Severn Sea white clouds raced out towards Devon. I came to Oxwich, beautiful for the limestone buttresses of its cliffs. Buzzards switchbacked in the high winds, ravens croaked over the woods and a peregrine passed like an arrow. Here that delight among ferns, the rusty-back, adorned the crevices. Oxwich bay and dunes were now below me: a scene of infinite peace that mid-March day. I was grateful to see it so early in the year for this is a very popular holiday haunt later on.

After Oxwich I let the main road lead me inland and back again to the coast near Paviland Cave, where the skeleton of 'The Red Lady' was found by Dr William Buckland in 1823 and which is amongst our most cherished palaeolithic specimens. I had now reached one of the choicest parts of Gower; those altogether delightful, flat-topped Paviland cliffs that ask to be walked along or leapt along in the company of sea winds, gulls and the scent of gorse.

The tide was in and the caves wave-spumed and inaccessible. But did that matter? Sufficient to have savoured these earliest haunts of man, to have got the feel of this ancient place, to have sat in the sun and imagined past scenes when the air was frigid, the sea further away and the caves looked out from a dry, raised platform onto an Arctic world which Paviland man shared with woolly rhinoceros, reindeer and other beasts whose bones were found with his in the caves. That day, as I looked across Gower to the shining snowfields of upland Carmarthenshire, the Arctic did not seem to have retreated very far.

But from these Paviland cliffs it is not to the north that you most naturally look. It is the west which pulls you, for now you see to the end of the peninsula. There is just enough curve in the coast to give you a glimpse of Worm's Head where it wriggles into the sea several miles away. And now if you want as heart-lifting a cliff-path

Worm's Head, at the western tip of Gower, becomes an island at high tide.

51

Gower's limestone cliffs near Worm's Head.

as you could desire you may walk those last miles to the end of Gower. Here in summer you may find a choice collection of limestone plants, including the very rare small restharrow, the equally rare goldilocks, the hoary rockrose and the spiked speedwell: all good reasons for making these cliffs worthy of their status of National Nature Reserve.

By the time I reached the end of the peninsula the tide had ebbed and I could walk over the rocks to the promontory, for this shapely Worm is an island at flood-tide. Never have I seen such millions of small mussels as clothe the rocks of this isthmus. For nearly half a mile they are your carpet and you crunch empty shells underfoot. No wonder curlews, oystercatchers and turn-stones rose in flocks before me as I stumbled across.

This extended finger of Gower ends in a fine hard chunk of limestone that drops sheer into the sea. I found a wide view from the top: south to Devon, west to St Govan's Head in Pembroke-shire, north to the mouth of the Tywi and beyond. But the finest panorama was the Gower itself when I looked back: the wide, wild curve of Rhossili Bay with a recently stranded ship sitting high up the beach in witness of the force of winter gales; then beyond, alluring sand-dunes stretching away up the Loughor estuary and meeting the wide sands of Llanrhidian. Here a Victorian guide-book of mine gives a visible shudder and speaks of this north-west corner as 'a desolate and ugly district infested with blown-sand burrows'. In other words just the place to make for if you like unspoilt places where plants and animals can still enjoy their natural haunts in peace.

As I sat contemplating that final, best bit of Gower, the sinking sun reminded me that it was over a mile back to the mainland and that unless I wanted a cold and hungry night on a wave-lapped rock I had better hurry back across the isthmus. Already Lundy's slow light was winking away in the south-west and by the time I had clambered up the mainland cliff and looked back the tides had met over the rocks and the great black hump of Worm's Head was again an island.

(1958)

SEABIRDS ABOUNDING

Our off-shore islands are slow to change but their bird populations are ever fluctuating. In the hope that it may have some archival interest, I have left this account of Skomer just as I wrote it in January, 1959, on the occasion of the island being given National Nature Reserve status.

Whichever way I have gone into the western extremities of Pembrokeshire my feelings have been the same: always the exciting sense of a strong land shaping itself ahead of me, of greater winds singing in the wires down the narrowing lanes, of barer fields and widening skies as the sea got closer. And then, coming clear of roads, walls and fields at last, there has been the final exhilaration of great promontories where gales thunder past your ears, and you look down at long lines of rollers moving steadily in below, breaking and cascading over the rocks, boiling through natural arches or spuming up through blow-holes. If this were all it would be satisfying enough.

But these extended claws of the land are not the last of Pembrokeshire. For where they grasp into the Atlantic round the beautiful bay of St. Brides, there are three islands: Ramsey, off the north arm of the bay, and Skomer and Skokholm off the south arm. And grouped about them are a host of smaller islets, rocks and skerries, many of them bearing, like these three, Scandinavian names that date back to their Viking settlers of eleven or twelve centuries ago.

Of these islands, Skomer, now being purchased by the Nature Conservancy with the co-operation of the West Wales Field Society, is the largest, being nearly two miles long and a mile and a half across. It is also nearest to the mainland, so near in fact, as you approach it along the road from Haverfordwest, it looks like a far extending peninsula, and not till you have walked up through the brambles and bracken onto the shoulder of the Deer Park headland, and

looked across Jack Sound, do you realise that nearly half a mile of dangerously rocky, tide-harrassed channel lies between you and what appears to be Skomer. But here appearances are deceptive to the end, for even if you could get across Jack Sound you would merely find yourself on the 20-acre islet of Middleholm, and still 100 yards of shallow sea from Skomer.

Therefore, as with most of the islands off Wales, the boat's way is far longer than the gull's. To get to Skomer you push your boat off the narrow stony beach of Martinshaven (facing north and secure in most winds) and if the sea is reasonable, and the outboard motor does not cough into silence more than once or twice, you can expect to feel the pebbles of Skomer under your feet within one hour. From there you can climb up the Neck, a triangular peninsula joined to Skomer by the narrowest of links; or you can ascend to the island's main plateau, in the centre of which stands the old deserted farmhouse unsheltered by any tree, and facing the four winds like a fortress. From here you may get your bearings, and set off to explore the island. And if you are unused to these bleak off-shore islands of the west your first impression may be discouraging. For even at the height of spring the flora at a distance may seem to be mainly a light green, rather stunted growth of bracken, and the birds few. But have faith; for though this island is bleak, the wild plants, though there is nothing rare, are surprisingly diverse; and the birds are there, 100,000 pairs of them, but out of your sight as yet and mostly out of your hearing, hidden in the cliffs below the plateau. For of all the Welsh islands, Skomer is by far the richest in birds.

Take the puffins, for instance. There may be as many puffins on Skomer as there are in the rest of England and Wales. The burrows of their towns spread far along the slopes and are estimated to house at least 100,000 inhabitants.

Wonderful to watch are their colourful assemblies on land and water and their mass flights along the cliffs. And as if this puffin multitude were not enough to amaze the visitor there are the great auk throngs of the sheer cliffs. Here, packed in lines along the most open dangerous ledges, are the inquisitive, neck-craning, head-bowing, squabbling, deep-voiced guillemots, whose groans and growlings come in successive gusts of sound along the cliffs. Skomer may house 5,000 pairs of guillemots; and with them almost as many razorbills. Add to these multitudes an increasing horde of large gulls, which in all may number 2,000 clangorous pairs; something like that number of kittiwakes; and then (numerically insignificant after these) about twenty-five other species, including peregrine, short-eared owl, buzzard, pheasant and perhaps occasionally chough.

Large colonies of kittiwakes breed on Skomer's cliffs.

But having seen all these you will not have seen every wonder of this fine sanctuary. In fact you will have missed what to many would be the chief marvel of the place, and which if you go only on a day-trip you certainly would miss. I mean the shearwaters. You can sail under those crowded cliffs and walk all over the island and never see a shearwater. For by day they are under your feet, incubating their round white eggs in long burrows, which they enter and leave only by night. So if you want to experience this crowning wonder of Skomer you must spend a night on the island, and hear the weirdly screaming chorus of uncountable thousands of shearwaters as they come in from the sea.

Then there are the mammals. Lost in delight at the birds, you might well miss some of the island's most interesting mammals. But there are two which force themselves on your notice, the seals and the rabbits. We on the west coast tend to take our grey seals so much for granted that we rarely appreciate them for what they are: one of the rarest seal species in the world. In Wales the Pembrokeshire coast and islands are the grey seal's strongholds, and a large proportion of the total population of Welsh seals is born on the beaches or in the caves of Ramsey and Skomer.

The seals, we may suppose, have always been there. The rabbits are an introduction, though what men first put them there is uncertain. We may guess that they date from Norman times and that they were introduced with the express intention of using the island as a rabbit-warren, as well as the sea-bird farm it already was. And there the rabbits have presumably persisted ever since and, just managing to survive the myxomatosis plague of 1955, they will soon be as multitudinous as ever, there being no predatory mammals to keep them in check.

Other Skomer wild mammals are woodmouse, common shrew, pygmy shrew and bank-vole; and this bank-vole has brought Skomer more fame in the world of science than all the other fauna put together. For this little red-backed scuttler in Skomer's grass, *Clethrionomys skomerensis*, is something unique in the world; it is a redder bank-vole than its mainland neighbours (from which it must have been cut off for many thousands of years) and is much bigger and tamer.

Much more could be written about Skomer. I have said nothing of the migrant birds, nothing of the few amphibians and reptiles, nor the insects, nor the teeming shore and off-shore life. And I have said too little of the vegetation which is richest in the cool, damp gullies and slopes of the north and east sides of the island, where in spring there is a succession of colour from the white of scurvy-grass and sea-campion, through the purple-blue sheets of bluebells and clumps of pale-yellow primroses to the differing pinks of thrift and red campion. These are the showy species. There are many others less conspicuous, less exciting to the casual plant-seeker but deeply interesting if you want to know why plants grow where they do. I am nearly forgetting the squill *Scilla verna*, a local plant of the west and north of Britain, and almost confined in Wales to the headlands and islands, and to be seen in May as a blue haze on the higher parts of Skomer where rabbits have nibbled the grass into a close sward while leaving the squills untouched.

And the future of this rich island? Nature Reserve status should assure the continued existence of its flora and fauna. At the least there should be no direct disturbance of this sanctuary. But there are other possible dangers to sea-birds, the greatest being that of oil. It is known that the numbers, particularly of auks, are declining fast; and the discharging of waste bilge-oil into the sea is almost certainly the major cause of this. With the current development of Milford Haven as an oilport one cannot help feeling uneasy for the teeming sea-bird populations of those islands, of which Skomer is one, that lie just outside the mouth of the Haven. It is to be hoped that no trouble will be spared in combating this terrible menace.

(1959)

PLANT-HUNTING ON CADER IDRIS

I like the way Camden's *Britannia* introduced its eighteenth-century readers to Merioneth and Cader Idris: 'At the back of Montgomeryshire lies Merionethshire . . . The prospects are both romantic and diversified, a mixture of high mountains and inaccessible rocks, innumerable rivers, cataracts, lakes, hills, woods, plains and some fertile valleys. Cader Idris is probably one of the highest mountains in Britain and, which is one certain argument of its height, affords some variety of alpine plants'.

In truth, far from being such a giant, Cader falls short of 3,000 feet and is not even the highest mountain in Merioneth. But 'some variety of alpine plants' is still there, and, even if they are easily outnumbered and outclassed by those of many other mountains, at least Cader has some historical prestige, for in the days when travel was difficult, and the remoter mountains were still undiscovered, Cader was almost sacred ground for botanists. Botanists are still doing excellent work there today and the mountain, thank heaven, is now a nature reserve.

If all you want is a mountain scramble you can make your way up Cader from any point of the compass, but I would prescribe the route from the north-east as the best for botanists. And no plant-hunter will be surprised to learn that this is the most tortuous, the most bog-trotting and the least likely to get you to the top. For this route you start from some high point on the old mountain road that links Dolgellau with Cross Foxes. From here you look across a tract called Tir Stent, a broken reach of semi-wooded slopes climbing away in wide, shallow steps towards open moorland with the Cader precipices beyond.

You leave the road and take to the bogs. Let us suppose it is the third week of June, when the green freshness of the spring has faded in the valleys but on the hills the year is still new. You climb gently from one wet terrace to the next, noting in some rather a dearth of colour (the very acid bogs), in others a massed gaiety of pale-pink or white heath spotted orchids, but little else (the less acid places); and here and there is a terrace that clearly cradles a richer earth, for quite suddenly you are among the crowded yellow heads of globe-flowers, or you are bending to admire varicoloured marsh orchids: small, deeply coloured purpurellas with diamond-shaped lips; the pale, pinched flowers of the incarnatas, with here and there a brick-red one; the sharply tapered spikes of the wood spotted orchids; and both the butterfly orchids.

For a mile or two these little saucers of bog and marsh are circled with thorn, oak and sycamore; but gradually the trees thin and eventually you come up to a ridge from which, as so often happens in mountains, you see you must descend before you can begin the final ascent. So down you scramble across a wide wet valley and in doing so you cross a road, though admittedly a road so rush-grown and sunk into the bog you might easily miss it. And though you may not be moved by ancient trackways, being intent on your plant-hunting, yet I would draw your attention to the botanical value of this partly-paved pony track that used to link mediaeval Dolgellau with the world beyond the mountains. Stoop and look, for instance, at the humble toad-rush and speculate on what boots or what hoofs in what century first brought its seeds along this way. Or put your nose over the fence and sniff carefully at the flowery alp alongside; for it is not only an abundance of fragrant orchids that makes the air so scented, but also the presence there of that aromatic and strangely-named plant, the spignel, meu or baldmoney. Now as this soft-leaved, white-flowered umbellifer is decidedly a northener, this Cader meadow being its most southern British locality, it may well be an introduction here. So probably it is no coincidence that a mile and a half away lies Gwanas, the site of a medieval hospice, and that this medieval road skirts the field in which the spignel grows.

Between this forgotten road and the cliffs of Cader itself there is little to detain you. The bogs get poorer (except for one which later in the year will be patched pale-blue with the minute, delicate cups of the ivy-leaved bell-flower and where you may find that rarity in Wales, the bog orchid); the soils get thinner and more and more rock begins to show. Here are heather and gorse, heath-rush and purple moor-grass: the flora of poverty. Across such ground you come under the cliffy ramparts of the mountain itself. And here it is possible your spirits may droop a little as your gaze travels round and up and down those great walls. For from the green bracken slopes at the foot, across ledges whiskery with heather and bilberry, right to the broken skyline at the top, it all looks as acid and unpromising as the ground under your feet or the scree beside you.

But have faith. The treasures of our alpine flora are rarely visible from afar, but must be sought for in chimney, crack and gully. So avoid the great, dry, bouldery scree: it is wearying to cross and will yield you little but bright-green fronds of parsley fern. Work round it to where a spring seeps down through a finer, wetter scree, and there you will find white-starred mats of mossy saxifrage and the tiny pink trumpets of that wondrous mountain-invader, the New Zealand willow-herb, looking as at home, among these stones, as if it had been here 2,000 years instead of twenty. And you might look for the alpine enchanter's nightshade, too. It would be a new plant for Cader Idris, but it grows on just such a scree under Aran Fawddwy only ten miles away, so why not here?

Once at the top of this scree you can look intimately at vertical rocks at last. Facing north, with half a thousand feet of cliff overshading them, they never feel the sun and are the first to see the snow: which makes them ideal for ferns, and here the crannies are full of brittle bladder-ferns, beech and oak ferns, filmy ferns,

polypodies and common and green spleenworts. The alpines come quickly after that. Over your head and most conspicuous, the roseroot thrusts out its yellow-flowered, fleshy-leaved stems from inaccessible crevices. At your feet, especially where water splashes down, are the attractive rosettes of starry saxifrage leaves, perfect setting for their white-petalled, red-anthered flowers. And at your eye-level, along the ledges, three fine species: the frail, slender fronds of lesser meadow-rue; the satisfying round leaves and distinguished-looking spikes of mountain sorrel; and the typically Welsh mountain variety, *cambrica*, of the golden-rod, a plant that looks quite different from common golden-rod, being shorter and stockier and flowering many weeks earlier (in fact, surely deserving to be called a separate species?).

Then if you are used to the Welsh poppy only in lowland gardens you may be surprised to see it perfectly at home up here on these mountain ledges. And there are other plants here you may have always thought of as lowlanders, species like wood anemone, primrose, meadow-sweet, rosebay willow-herb, early purple orchid and ox-eye daisy. For some of these Cader plants you must go later than June to see them at their best. For one of them you must go months earlier, for it is early in the year that the purple saxifrage— perhaps the finest of our alpines if only because it is in March (sometimes even mid-February) that it glows out in full bloom, amid east winds and icicles—astonishes the winter mountaineer. And one last word about alpines: if you do visit Cader, look hard for the pink flowers of the moss campion. It was described in the 1920s as extinct on Cader but it is, in fact, still there, though extremely rare at this its most southerly British station.

So, slowly, you work your way up. It is not necessary to rock-climb, for there are easy scrambling routes. And when you come up out of the cwm on to the moorland above, do not think that all that is left is grasses and club-mosses. For this once classical mountain keeps its best trick to the last. If you will spurn the top, and work your way round to the wide chimneys on the east side, you will find there a genista of some rarity, the hairy greenweed, which makes twiggy mats on a few of the rocks and covers itself with small yellow broom-like flowers. What is most odd is that in the hairy greenweed you have a plant which, in Britain, is mainly lowland and southern (near the sea in Cornwall and Pembrokeshire, for instance) and yet here on Cader, at its most northerly British locality, it is at its highest elevation by far: a most unusual state of affairs. In fact, so improbable did it seem to H.C. Watson, that, in his *Topographical Botany* of 1883, he wrote off the old Cader record of hairy greenweed as 'an error'. Less

than 20 years later it was re-discovered there 'in fine quantities' and so it remains today, looking from its high buttresses down on to Tal-y-llyn pass and the lake far below, surely one of the finest positions of any plant in Wales.

If there is one lost plant which, more than any other, needs re-finding on Cader Idris, it is the oblong woodsia, perhaps Britain's rarest fern. Known to survive further north in Snowdonia as well as in the Lake District and Scotland, this little fern was found twice on Cader in the late nineteenth century but never since. Has it now gone from Cader, wiped out by collectors or maybe by acid rain? How alpine botanists would love to know!

(1960)

Oblong woodsia, one of Britain's rarest ferns, was found on Cader Idris in the nineteenth century but not since.

TREASURE IN THE GORGE

I had long been curious to see that rarity, the Bristol rock-cress, especially since I learned that it was once reported from a range of hills in Radnorshire. Assuming that it really grew on those Carneddau uplands, I suppose it was always extremely rare there and once it got known it soon disappeared into collections. To remain undiscovered can sometimes be a rare plant's best hope of survival.

Having occasion to visit Somerset today I set off especially early, knowing from old experience how long some plants are in the finding, and I did not expect the Bristol rock-cress to be any exception. My way took me south to meet the spring by way of the Wye valley and so to Glofter (as Gloucester is still delightfully spelt on the old turnpike milestones). I drove mile after mile through all the delicate and varied greens, yellows and reds of the spring trees: green of sycamore leaves, yellow of wych elm seed-discs, rich red-purple curtains of poplar catkins. Along the new motorway near Ross I saw where the road has been cut through wild daffodil country. There are quantities of daffodils in the fields on either hand and there are other daffodils springing up on the raw red clay of the new road-banks and on the central division between the traffic lanes. Could anything be more joyous? But will they who administer the weed-killing poisons of tidy-minded officialdom think so too?

By early afternoon I was looking into that great limestone trench that is the Avon gorge and feeling grateful to the friend who had told me exactly where I might find the rock-cress, for in that vast place I could have searched haphazardly for a week and not seen it. As it was I soon found it in the scree of an abandoned quarry among the trees, just a few plants inconspicuously white-flowered but a little taller, showier, more elegant than I had expected in a cress. Most of the plants were in full bloom but some already bristled with long, narrow, upward pointing seed pods. Near it, almost touching it, grew another endearing and rare crucifer, hutchinsia, its tiny white flowers also getting a little over, some of its leaves brown and autumnal. Lots of the fingered saxifrage everywhere and, final delight, that curious dwarf, little-known umbellifer, the honewort, its white flowers already beginning to open in this early spring. The steep woods were full of beauty with the wych elms gloriously yellow among the naked ash trees, and hawthorns an exciting green along the rim of the gorge. Many yews grow with natural grace along the slopes and ilexes seed themselves freely in the clearings. What was new to me was to see the rusty-back, most charming of the small ferns, growing naturally in scree. For though this is quite a common little fern in our part of Wales we know it mainly at artificial sites such as lime-mortared walls. Incidentally, a strange use is recorded for this fern in Anglesey: Holyhead men used it as a bait for sea-fishing though I cannot imagine what fish they caught with it. But as it has such a colourful underside it could, I suppose, have been trailed through the water as a spinning lure, perhaps.

(1961)

59

IN THE STEPS OF THE ROMANS

Nearly 2,000 years ago the Roman city of Viroconium was a vital centre of West Midland communications, as nearby Shrewsbury is to-day. Bold roads struck out of it to radiate the Roman power to the four horizons. One went north to Chester; one east to London; a third south to Caerleon; a fourth west into central Wales. Of these roads it is this one to the west that is the least known, probably the least solidly made, certainly the hardest to find as it picks its way shyly through the fields and over the hills of Wales, getting ever more faint and fragmentary until . . . But let me tell you the whole story as far as I know it.

You start at Viroconium (Wroxeter). Among the excavated ruins of the baths you see chunks of masonry gathered in heaps and you admire Roman stones in the Saxon walls of the church near by. It is well to look carefully at these palpable relics of Romano-British life, for along the entire length of the road you will see almost nothing like them. Practically everything of the road and of its several forts lies underground, just as most of Viroconium still lies below wide fields of barley. The most you can hope to see of this road is the worn, humped shape that its agger, or raised causeway, still makes in the turf here and there.

Remains of the Roman town of Wroxeter, near Shrewsbury. From here the Romans probably had a westward road to their centres at Forden, Caersws, Cae Gaer and Trawsgoed.

It is debated whether the Romans used this east-west route along the ridge of the Long Mountain but it is certainly an ancient road.

I have never followed the road in detail along its 17 miles across Shropshire. That stretch is well enough known and I have always been anxious to get to the more mysterious Welsh part of it. You are not far from the road as you start off up the Shrewsbury by-pass and then glance off westwards through Meole Brace, passing close to the site of a Roman villa, then through a place significantly named Stony Stretton and so to the village of Westbury.

After Westbury the road climbs and climbs until it crosses the border into Wales. You are now on Long Mountain, at 1,100 ft above sea-level. From here the road turns south-west both to keep to the highest ground and to head straight for the Roman fort at Forden. Not that there seems anything very Roman about the road just here. In fact the experts now insist that the

Roman road went along the southern flank, not the summit ridge, of Long Mountain.

From Long Mountain the road, Roman or not, descends steeply to the wide vale of the Severn through a gap in Offa's Dyke. The modern road swings right, but the old road and the dyke go down through the fields together till they come to the Welshpool-Church Stoke road. Here Offa's Dyke turns sharply off southwards and you are left wondering what has happened to the ancient road. For across the main road where it should logically go you see nothing but a dull, unhelpful-looking pasture with a solitary oak in the middle. You lean on the gate, gazing at this problematical pasture, looking in vain for even a nebulous trace of an agger on its surface. But look again at that mid-field oak. It is old and remembers farther back than you by two or three centuries. And see, now, that directly between it and your gate are the stools of two other ancient oaks. So a hedge once probably crossed the field along that line, a hedge along the road maybe. You look away beyond and see that in the next field a still existing hedge continues the alignment of these oaks and that there is a gateway there just where it ought to be. That way, all agree, the Roman road went. Yet no agger is perceptible under the broad light of the midday sun. But do what I chanced to do. Return that way in the evening, when the sun's rays are level across the field, and then you will quite easily see a shadowy line on the golden turf, the agger of the Roman road going straight down the field past the oak to the gate at the far end.

From there, by old hedges and ancient gateways, the road goes straight over several fields to stop short at a churchyard wall. For Forden church evidently stands square on the Roman road. Beyond the church the road goes on down the hill and fords the Camlad river, beyond which a long straight hedge marks it onward right to the Severn-side Roman fort called Forden Gaer, now a rectangular field perched 6 ft above its neighbours and dropping to them down a bank still steep, firm and entire. West of Forden Gaer the road goes as straight as the Severn allows for Newtown, somewhat as A483 goes today. But four-and-a-half miles beyond Newtown, where the main road makes a slight deflection to the left, you will see that a faint but definite agger continues straight on through the fields alongside a hedge. In another mile it passes conspicuously through the grounds of Maesmawr Hall, whence it emerges straight, raised and obvious, following the remnant of a hedge, before it ends abruptly at the river bank, in full sight of the next Roman fort, Caersws.

Though Caersws is a Roman fort now mixed up with a village, you can still see Roman embankments by the railway station. In the walls of Llanwnog church, a mile north, you will find foreign-looking sandstone blocks that almost certainly came from Roman Caersws. And you can easily pick up the Roman road again two or three fields west of Caersws. Then it becomes a present-day lane for a few straight hundred yards to a house where the modern lane turns sharp right, leaving the Roman way to leap competently forwards up a low hill that takes it on nearly to the village of Trefeglwys. I stood on that hill one spring day trying vainly to detect the exact line of the road from there across the fields to Trefeglwys. The agger has long since been blurred by cultivation. Idly I listened to the larks and the peewits and watched a tractor ploughing and trailing a cloud of red dust and white gulls. Then, suddenly, I saw the tractor heave itself off the level of the field over an invisible hump. Fascinated, I watched the ploughman turn the headland and come back. Again in midfield the tractor rose and fell and again next time and every time, as long as I watched. And now it had been pointed out to me I could see very faintly but continuously the line of the ancient road spanning the field from hedge to hedge.

Immediately west of Trefeglwys the country gets stronger, higher, wilder. Ahead lies the forbidding mass of Plynlimon and the road begins to get awkward. Awkward because all the time you want to swing it to the left, as tradition and all reason at first suggest it should go, towards the next Roman fort at Cae Gaer, south of Plynlimon. But, instead, the road resists you, pushing you firmly to the right into the mouth of a narrowing valley that points you uncompromisingly towards the north, not the south, of Plynlimon. And having landed you in this valley with no hope of retreat the road fails you abruptly and you go on by faith and by guess until you come up at last to the ancient lead-mines at Dylife, a place that pretty certainly had Roman connections and that probably supplied the lead found during the excavations at Caersws.

Yet though you have got up to the Dylife moors and are, perhaps, even postulating a Roman road going on down the other side to the Roman fort at Pennal on the Dyfi, there is always that nagging little worry you left behind at Caersws—the problem of whether the Romans did or did not have a road-link with Cae Gaer, south of Plynlimon. It has been reasonably argued that Cae Gaer was a temporary, quite unimportant, site and so a road would never have been constructed to it. But this argument became less forceful when another Roman fort, large and looking important, was discovered at Trawsgoed, 11 miles straight on over the hills beyond Cae Gaer. Surely the Romans would have had a direct road-link from Caersws to Trawsgoed? And if so it must have gone via Cae Gaer. In fact, there is, heading west over the hills from Cae Gaer, an old road called the lead-miners' track. And no doubt that it is what it was, a nineteenth-century lead-miners' road. But may not other lead-miners have used that road, perhaps back in Roman times? For over in the west, along the Ystwyth river on whose banks Trawsgoed fort was built, are lead-mines of reputedly Roman origin.

Amid all these perplexities one thing is certain. For many years to come there will remain a great deal of patient but rewarding field-work to be done by archaeologists, amateur or professional, towards the unravelling of Roman-road mysteries. For the road I have described here is only one of many problematical roads across Wales.

(1961)

A 1958 view up the Tarennig valley to Plynlimon when the conifer plantations were young. The open space among the trees in the foreground is the site of Cae Gaer, a Roman camp. Road A44 goes up the valley at extreme right.

NIGHT ON A DESERT ISLAND

Since I first landed on Cardigan Island there have been significant changes. The rats have been destroyed; efforts have been made to attract breeding puffins and shearwaters; and there has been a numerous colonisation by lesser black-backed gulls.

It was on a sun-filled afternoon in late July, 1961, that I landed on Cardigan Island amid a clangour of anxious, aggressive herring gulls that swooped at me to protect their young ones crouching in the scurvy-grass along the cliff-top.

The sea was calm. The boat had swayed in the tide-race, but it slid smoothly in between the rocks of the island's landing creek and let me jump out with my tent and my rucksack. Then it backed out gently, turned its bows towards the mainland, and in a minute was gone round the point, leaving me alone to explore the island.

As every new island should, this one had several quick surprises for me. First there was the lushness of the grass. From the mainland the island had looked burnt and thirsty, but now I found that the brownness that capped the whole top of this cliffy island was due only to the heavy seeding of the grasses. For the grass itself was deep and springy and lovely to polish your feet on. That, and a complete absence of gorse, inspired my first act: I cast off my sandals to give my feet 24 hours' freedom.

My second surprise was to find a natural well, for the boatman had told me that no one had ever lived or ever could live permanently on Cardigan Island because there is no drinking water.

My third surprise was to find the clear traces of earth walls in straight lines and curves that suggested the fields of some far antiquity. Then on top of one of the island's two hills there was what seemed the remains of a tumulus or some other sort of man-raised mound. Finally, an unpleasant find: there were rat-holes, dozens of them, round the cliff-tops wherever there was

Cardigan Island from the south-west.

earth soft for burrowing, enough to chill any hope of finding puffins or shearwaters breeding there, for it is particularly those birds that nest in holes that are preyed on by rats.

How, I wonder, did the dreadful brown rats get on to this otherwise delectable island? Could they have swum across from the mainland, attracted by the smell of the island's bird cliffs? For at the lowest tides the channel narrows from 200 yards to less than half that distance. If you doubt that rats are so enterprising you may prefer the shipwreck theory, in support of which I can offer you the 6,500-ton liner *Herefordshire,* which was being towed from the Dart to the breakers' yards in the Clyde. She tore adrift from her tugs in heavy seas on 15 March, 1934, and was deposited by a north-west gale on to the north-west corner of the island. She clung to the rocks, so I was told, long enough for any number of rats to get ashore and then quietly slid into the sea, where she lies to this day in no great depth of water.

Let me give you a few of the island's measurements. The length east to west is just under half a mile; the breadth just less than a quarter-mile; it is almost completely surrounded by sheer cliffs, but none is much higher than about 100 ft.

There are a number of caves at sea-level, but I could not climb down into them to see how far they extended. Some of the rock is beautifully gnarled and honeycombed and so shattered and contorted that the earth must have gone through some agonising moments producing it. Of the two high points (you rise only gently to them from the flattish top of the rest of the island), the higher is 172 ft, the other (where my alleged tumulus is) being a few feet lower.

In my 24 hours there I walked right round the island several times. I listed all the birds I saw (there were 24 species) and all the plants I could find (some 40 different sorts). Besides gulls there were shags and a few cormorants and oyster-catchers nesting; a fulmar flew close round the island; six kittiwakes stood on the north cliffs,

five adults and one young one. I saw gannets, razorbills and guillemots off-shore.

Three kinds of bird sang: skylark, rock pipit and meadow pipit. The crow tribe was well represented: dozens of jackdaws and a pair each of ravens, carrion crows and choughs. Earlier this century puffins used to nest on the island, but as from some other Welsh islands they have now gone. (Enter rats, exit puffins?) I lay awake till after midnight and woke several times before dawn hoping to hear night birds such as owls or shearwaters, but there were none.

The other living creatures were a mixed bag. There were a few grasshoppers, woodlice and ladybirds. I saw three kinds of butterfly: meadow brown, small copper and grayling; and there were six-spot burnet moths. In the sea there were seals that quietly watched me all day, and once a score of dolphins rolled and leapt among the white-topped green breakers a few yards from the rocks. Finally there were the sheep: 21 small, nearly black, horned sheep called Soays, a primitive breed said to date back to the Vikings who introduced them to some of the Scottish islands. The flock on Cardigan Island was put there a few years ago by the West Wales Field

Soay sheep, a primitive breed, were put on Cardigan Island by the West Wales Field Society.

Looking across the narrow sound from Cardigan Island to the mainland cliffs.

Society. Soays may be the nearest we have to true wild sheep in north Europe and wild their behaviour remains, for they went bounding off to the other end of the island whenever they saw me. It was only by the use of a telephoto lens that I was able to get anything of a photograph of them.

So there was one animal of distinction—this fine-horned, ibex-like primitive sheep grazing on what are perhaps the fields of primitive man. For a bird of distinction I would choose the choughs whose cheerful voices woke me soon after dawn. A plant of distinction? Yes, I think two: first the vernal squills that must have been a sheet of blue in May and which had now gone to seed. For my

second plant I would choose the tree mallow, a splendid species that belongs so much to the islands, even the isolated stacks, of our rocky western coasts and is often, as on Cardigan Island, the only plant that gets anywhere near to being a tree, growing tall and rather woody and producing large leaves and big pink flowers in defiance of all the salt sea-winds that blow.

That night I unrolled my sleeping-bag on a soft bed of grass in a hollow circled by a low bank that I like to think was a hut-circle. But even if it was no such thing, some one had made it and I am sure a very long time ago. For a while I sat in the still warm dusk watching the four bright flashes of Strumble light 18 miles to the south-west. But Bardsey's light, which I had hoped would shine nearly 50 miles to the north, was either lost in cloud or too low on the horizon to be visible. Then I lay awake under the stars watching the play of the grasses close to my face and hearing the very softest swish of wind through grass, the very slightest rustle of water against rock: sounds you miss in the daytime.

Waking in the night I heard oystercatchers piping to one another, the calls of passing redshanks and the occasional unaccountable alarms of the gulls rising up in sudden shouting bursts into the dark sky, then slowly subsiding. I also heard a gnawing close to my ear and discovered that a rat had got into my rucksack and was helping itself to a packet of sandwiches.

When I woke in the morning as the choughs called and bounced through the air over me I was conscious first of grasses shaking wildly against racing grey clouds. There was an autumnal touch in the light twitter of passing finches. I felt the wind stronger over the island and heard a heavier

sea than that of the previous night. I stood up to see white water breaking all round the rocks and spray flying far. I looked at the creek, the one possible landing place in this island of rocks, and saw the waves surging heavily into it. If it was like this on what was merely a breezy summer day, what, I asked myself, was it like in winter?

By the afternoon, when the tide had ebbed, the waves fell a little and when the boat came I was able to fling my pack and then myself into it. Quickly on the south-flowing tide we slipped through the narrow sound. We looked up at the cliffs, at the south cliffs gasping with summer; at three young golliwogs of cormorants on a nest, their mouths agape and their throats vibrating to get air; at the sea-beet hanging great seeding heads from the ledges. Then the island was behind us and soon we were entering the Teifi river and our boat was dancing through the wavelets of the bar.

(1961)

Herring gulls and shags at the western tip of Cardigan Island, 1961.

MAY-DAY RITES

Many a cottage gateway, especially in the Celtic parts of the British Isles, is watched over by a pair of rowan trees. Set on each side of the gate they were bent together in infancy to form an arch. They grew into each other's branches and eventually married as trees will, their trunks flowing into each other to become one and indivisible. Seeing this happy union (if they lived to see it) their planters rejoiced at the fulfilment of their design; for now their defences were complete and no evil spirit, no malignant enchantment, could get into their garden or house. In so arching rowans over their gate they had followed a Celtic custom dating back to the remotest times we have any inkling of.

A pair of weather-beaten old rowan trees arched over the gateway of an abandoned Welsh farmhouse to protect the former inhabitants from misfortune.

There have been other trees useful against witchcraft—ash, hawthorn, holly, elderberry—but rowan has always been the favourite. If you were wise you took a rowan-stick to fetch in the cattle (carrying it in your left hand), you hung it carefully in the cowshed during milking and you drove the cows back to pasture with it afterwards. By so doing you ensured that no disease would afflict your stock. As a further precaution you hung a bunch of rowan twigs outside the cow-house door. For a cream-stirrer you used a rod of rowan but woe betide your cream if you stirred it with your right hand! In late summer you gathered the berries and made rowan-beer (what potion more effective for drinking your friends' health?) or rowan-wine, which was strongly medicinal and whose use in Welsh mountain districts has only recently died out in favour of stuff from the chemists. (In some places, however, perhaps where the power of rowan used to be more feared than loved, the berries were held to be poisonous.)

So the wiles of the elfin and other mischievous folk were forfended round the year. But there was one day when rowan-rites were specially celebrated and that was the first day of May. Then it was that you made hoops of the wood and in the morning and again in the evening you caused the sheep and lambs to pass through them. Why the first of May? Because that was regarded as the most dangerous time of the year, more critical even than the midwinter and midsummer solstices. For now spring was resurgent, the earth was radiating powerful, life-giving forces and supernatural influences were rampant.

Direct contact with these life-giving forces was held to be extremely hazardous. You worshipped but at the same time dreaded them. Especially in the hawthorn was the spirit of vegetation revered but though you picked sprigs of may-blossom you did not bring them into the house: that would have invited disaster. It was a time of year to veil yourself from the direct rays of the sun; and you kept a tight hold on your rowan-stick because of the witches.

For May-day not only released the elemental forces of fertility in man, animal and plant: it regenerated the powers of the witches also. For on May-day Eve (Walpurgis Night) they sallied forth full of a zest understandable on the opening of the spell-casting season and many the luckless man and beast who was bewitched on that fateful night. In the north-east of Scotland, as no doubt elsewhere in the Celtic world, witchcraft was countered on May-day by burning fires of rowan branches. In building such fires any part of the tree had to be kept on the left side of the body. The fires were lit on the hills round every village and in front of every cottage, so affording a double circle of defence against the invading magic. This May-day festival of Beltane was common to all Celtic nations.

Intimately connected with protection by fire was the idea of purification. To walk between two fires on May-day or to leap through the flames was wholesome for man and beast alike. These rites were not extinct in the Scottish Highlands until early last century. The beginning of May also saw the rite of extinguishing all household fires so that they could be relit amid great ceremony from the needfire, the sacred bonfire kindled on Beltane Day. Each domestic fire, kept burning for the following twelve months, thus became a minor tutelary power.

Long after the arrival of Christianity the fear of elemental forces still stretched a vast hand over the Celtic world. Though their meaning gradually faded, the legends of the dark past remained like shadows in the background of people's memories, ominous and disquieting. Unable to dispel the old superstitions and end the ancient rites the Church often found it necessary to Christianise them by linking them with ecclesiastical festivals. Christian fire-rites were long practised in many European countries and still persist on St. John's Eve (midsummer) in parts of the Continent.

It is strange how, out of all these fear-racked May-days of the past, there gradually evolved something altogether agreeable: the traditional 'Merrie England' May-day of the Middle Ages when contented villagers tripped lightly on the green and went through cheerful rites whose dark origin they had little or no idea of. All they knew was that on the first day of May you must rise before dawn to go a'maying in the woods and that you returned before sunrise, your arms full of may and wildflowers for decorating the outside (only) of your cottage. Then you decked a pole with streamers and passed the day dancing round it and in other frolics such as morris dancing led by such traditional figures as Robin Hood and Maid Marian.

Perhaps you wonder how often may-blossom was out by May-day, for even in mild districts this is an early date? But remember that prior to the revision of our calendar in 1752, when eleven days were taken out, May-day fell nearly a fortnight later than it does now and almanacs from then on showed two May-days, the Old and the New. Perhaps, too, you may wonder at the simple enthusiasm of people for these celebrations?

Certainly it is hard for most of us today, urbanised and sophisticated by two centuries of industrial revolution, to imagine folks joyously rising in a cold dawn of spring to gather nosegays and garlands. But there is no doubt of the universality of this delightful custom, as witness in Shakespeare's *Henry the Eighth* the door-keeper's words when he tried to disperse the crowd that gathered for the christening scene:

''Tis as much impossible
(Unless we sweep them from the door with
                                    cannons)
To scatter them, as 'tis to make them sleep
On May-day morning, which will never be.'

Never? So it must have seemed in Shakespeare's day.

(1962)

PLYNLIMON'S HASTENING RIVER

On a sparkling spring day, in search of skylarks and solitude, I went off to visit a favourite place of mine—Llyn Llygad Rheidol ('The Lake of the Rheidol's Source') which is tucked in under the western flank of Plynlimon (Pumlumon). I began by motoring up the long climbing valley that takes you south-east from Machynlleth to the hills. In my driving mirror I could see the landscape building up higher and higher behind me across what Hilaire Belloc called one of the great unknown views of Britain, the 'awful trench which opens under your feet north and

Llyn Llygad Rheidol, source-lake of the Rheidol river, lies in a corrie on the western flanks of Plynlimon.

beyond Plynlimon'. The little road from Machynlleth lifts you steeply out of the trench to give you at the top of the pass a great view back to the whole of Cader Idris in the north, and a great view forward to all the billowing slopes, all the folded valleys of Plynlimon to the south. From here, if you are a walker, you can take to the grass and the heather and make your way quite gently along one of the finest ridge walks of Wales, till you come up to the highest of Plynlimon's several tops and look down at the crag-shadowed waters of the source-lake of the Rheidol.

In the breasts of our easily impressed forbears of a century or more ago, Plynlimon used to generate considerable awe. But the 'sublime' mountain of yesterday has been downgraded and now usually finds itself described not as a mountain but as elevated moorland. There are times when I would not call it a mountain either. So often have I splashed rather than walked over it that I would call Plynlimon a big wet sponge, a sponge holding in it untellable millions of gallons of acid water. For this reason Plynlimon is the mother of famous rivers—Wye and Severn flow off her eastern flanks; to the north she sends off tributaries to the Dyfi; and on the west she gives birth to the Rheidol. And while the Severn reaches the sea slowly, four counties and over two hundred miles away, the hasty Rheidol knows only Cardiganshire and is in the sea in little more than twenty miles.

There is something rather strange about the name Rheidol. I am not thinking of its etymology: that tricky matter is one for the experts to wrestle with. You will see what puzzles me if you follow the new-born river from the source-lake where it rushes down its first cleft in the mossy, grassy moorland. After just a mile this very juvenile stream flows into a much broader one, the Hengwm, which rises high up on the north end of Plynlimon and is already

The dam of Nant-y-moch reservoir under construction in 1961 along the upper reaches of the Rheidol.

nearly four miles long by the time the Rheidol joins it. Yet from that confluence onwards, though the Rheidol is clearly only a tributary of the Hengwm, the word Rheidol takes over and the Hengwm is forgotten. But in the naming of rivers such inconsistencies are not rare.

The enormous liberality with which British mountains make and store rain made water seem cheap stuff to our ancestors. But man's ideas change and now water, even the remotest mountain water, is a coveted liquid to be piped and stored and used to turn the wheels of industry or slake the thirst of distant towns. So in the 1960s the quiet high valleys under the west of Plynlimon were invaded by hydro-electric engineers who gathered all the waters of the upper Rheidol and its side-streams and im-

pounded them in a great reservoir, so flooding a moorland valley that was once the haunt of pipits, snipe, short-eared owls and sheep; and drowned with the valley was the sheep farm of Nant-y-moch which for many years had been the highest occupied house in the district. Nant-y-moch's last occupants were men whom ethnologists believed may have been directly blood-linked with the prehistoric inhabitants of these parts, the shadowy beings who far back in the long unfolding of the years raised the once huge but now dilapidated cairns on Plynlimon and who dropped the little flint arrowheads that are still occasionally to be picked up in the peat.

For many years the Plynlimon uplands had been getting less and less populous. They had lain remote and unvisited except by shepherds

71

and occasional walkers and horse-riders. But this century in mid-Wales we have seen a great opening up of access roads for new forests and new reservoirs. The unknown valleys of yesterday have become the coach-trip routes of today. So it was with Elan, Vyrnwy, Claerwen and after them, Rheidol, bringing an end to peace and wildness.

From Nant-y-moch the Rheidol flows another four moorland miles south to its first village, Ponterwyd. They are four miles of unhappy history, for they contain a concentration of former lead-mines that infamously polluted the Rheidol in the last century. By the 1950s the river had slowly cleaned itself and had been restocked with fish. Then came the hydroelectric scheme. Biologists and anglers were quick to foresee the probability that the flooding of old lead workings might unleash another era of pollution. To meet these fears the engineers undertook extensive measures to keep lead out of the river.

At Ponterwyd the Rheidol flows under its first main-road bridge, an unbeautiful iron thing which compares ill with the still-existing shapely old stone bridge it superseded. Then below Ponterwyd the river flows its seven or eight most famous miles. Here it seems to find a softer rock and has cut deep. It begins to lead a life of its own down between the walls of a ravine overhung by steep woodlands. Soon you can get to the river only by narrow paths that zigzag you down through two hundred feet of bilberries, spindly oaks and birches. And even when you are at the bottom of the path, as at Parson's Bridge, the river is still far below you, boiling along in its deep slot, forcing itself between carved walls and eddying in wonderfully smoothed and rounded potholes.

The oakwoods in the gorge above Devil's Bridge are not the finest oakwoods in the world. Thin acid soils clinging desperately to precipitous gorge-sides do not produce great trees, and it is probable that not in all history has man been tempted to get at this poor and scarcely accessible timber. That he has had plenty of time to do so had he wished is proved by his ancient remains hereabouts. What look like prehistoric stones still stand in the churchyard wall at Ysbyty Cynfyn above Parson's Bridge and, much less easy to find, especially among the summer bracken, is the Bronze Age stone circle across the river on the hillside of Bryn Bras. Wholly unexploited woodlands are very rare in Britain, but these Rheidol woods come as near as any to being virgin. As such they are prized by botanists and are now a National Nature Reserve.

You should not go to Devil's Bridge in summer unless you wish to share its waterfalls, its turnstiles, its cafés, its stony staircases, its bridges and grottoes with car-loads, bus-loads, even train-loads of people. But on most days in winter and early spring you can muse there as solitary as Wordsworth did a century and a half ago. The difficulty is to force yourself to go on down-river from Devil's Bridge, so refreshing is this upland country, so little inhabited, so nearly primeval. The temptation is to stay and admire, to enjoy the cool shade of the gorges, to explore, to botanise or to watch the frequent kites, buzzards, grey wagtails and pied flycatchers. The plant-seeker, especially, may be pleasantly surprised. Near Parson's Bridge, for instance, there comes down the gorge-side an unexpected belt of calcareous rock that brings a welcome enrichment of the vegetation. The general poverty of the flora suddenly gives place to an outbursting of primroses, marjoram, hard shield-fern, tutsan, meadow saxifrage and other choice plants including that rarity, Forster's stonecrop. It was plants from the Rheidol gorge that first gave Forster the idea that this stonecrop was something new.

Then there is the lure of the tributaries, especially Afon Mynach over which the famous triple bridges of Devil's Bridge are straddled. Follow the Mynach upstream and you will find two miles up that it divides among the Forestry plantations into a pair of hurrying streams, which lead you back into the hills to high waterfalls that come pouring down heathery rocks into deep green pools.

At Devil's Bridge the Rheidol, so far a southing stream all the way, now turns abruptly west, having been captured, as some geologists say, by a stream that ages ago bit back into the Rheidol's course and diverted it down the nearest route to the sea. Before then the Rheidol may have flowed on southwards into what is now the valley of the Teifi. But that goes back to a landscape very different from today's.

From Devil's Bridge there are twelve miles to the sea. At first the valley is still deep and steep-sided, with a fair wealth of oak woodland. Then seven miles from the coast, where the valley begins to flatten, the river was dammed to create the lowest of the three hydro-electric reservoirs. Soon the Rheidol flows out into its final stretch. For the first time its banks are flat fields, between which it has changed its course for centuries, as you may see from the quiet backwaters that lie a quarter of a mile from the present river and are the paths of its former meanders. This is a peaceful, pastoral vale, with the Rheidol low and clear and rippling between wide pebble-washes, leaving the backwaters as tranquil sanctuaries, where dabchicks and moorhens pop out of sight among pondweeds and waterlilies.

The river's name, like so many Celtic river names, may well be extremely ancient, going back to prehistoric days. In literature it is first mentioned, with the spelling Retiaul, in a

The old bridge over the Rheidol, Ponterwyd.

73

Where the Rheidol reaches the sea in Aberystwyth harbour. (A photograph of the 1950s).

twelfth-century life of St. Padarn, the most famous human name with which the river is associated. For Padarn founded in the sixth century the powerful monastery of Llanbadarn Fawr. The monastery disappeared many centuries ago but Llanbadarn, with its fine medieval church, long remained the most important place along the river. Today Aberystwyth has virtually swallowed Llanbadarn. But formerly, Aberystwyth, being castled, was merely Llanbadarn Gaerog, that is the fortified part of Llanbadarn. To go back farther: at Capel Bangor, just upstream from Llanbadarn, the great west road of Roman times crossed the Rheidol, linking the forts of Pennal and Trawsgoed. Some day perhaps someone will find its fording place in the river-bed. But it is unlikely, for the Rheidol has seen many floods; and just as its bridges have often been swept away, so its fords probably have been, too. As for the meaning of Rheidol, scholars are inclined to connect it with the Welsh *rhedeg*, to run. And what meaning can be more fitting for so impatient a river?

The Rheidol, far more than its neighbour the Ystwyth, is Aberystwyth's river, though the town is never likely to change its name to Aber-rheidol. It was on the Ystwyth's banks that the original Aberystwyth castle stood on a hilltop above the valley. The later castle was built on the Rheidol, but in moving north it took its old name with it. Around this second castle the medieval town developed. The Ystwyth and the Rheidol, which once had separate mouths, now come together in Aberystwyth harbour and there is an end of them. But not quite, maybe; for this coast has seen changes. Go a little north and see the stumps of a long-extinct forest sticking up from the sand at low tide, showing that where now is sea there was once land. And across that land the Rheidol and other rivers must have gone. So who shall deny the possibility that even today the channel of the ancient Rheidol still exists on the ocean bed, a furrow too faint to show on Admiralty charts but there all the same, winding through the ooze to some shadowy line that was the shoreline of long ago?

(1962)

74

MIXED FORTUNES OF THE LEAD-MINES

The very numerous old lead-mines of mid-Wales first attracted me as places where I might find some of the less usual bats, birds and wildflowers. In their ruinous walls I found wheatears, stock doves and kestrels breeding. Occasionally ravens would build high up on derelict machinery. Down one mine I saw the nest of a ring ouzel, and sometimes there was the excitement of watching choughs come plunging down the sky to vanish into the depths of a shaft. As for plants, though most of them shudder at the poisonous ground near lead-mines, there are a few that seem to prefer it. There is that rare little fern, the forked spleenwort, for instance; and alpine pennycress and vernal sandwort are also worth looking out for. Is it that in the mixture of minerals thrown up from the mines these plants find enough lime to keep them happy despite the lead?

As well as their special wildlife and minerals the mines are also rich in history and archaeology. Yet despite recent attempts to tidy

Vernal sandwort, a typical lead-mine plant in some parts of Britain.

Forked spleenwort, a rare fern often associated with lead-mines.

them up, a few of the mines remain dismal places surrounded by acres of grey spoil on which practically nothing will grow, even after a century of exposure to sun, wind and rain. It is when you see this dead and barren ground, and hear of rivers too poisonous for fish to live in and of fields too polluted for animals to graze on that you realise just how poisonous lead is. But to take in the final deadliness of lead you should go to the churchyards and look at miners' grave-stones to see at what early ages the dust-disease wrecked their lungs.

But perhaps you prefer the romantic side of industry? If so, you can get your imagination working on the mining past. Picture to yourself the laborious opening of the first tentative trenches of prehistoric time; then the slow cutting of shafts and adits ever deeper into the rock as time passed; the spurts of hopeful activity between long periods of abandonment and despair; the miners' camps and villages that have come and gone with the years.

Some of the mines of north and central Wales are credited with great antiquity. And why not, when even Caesar in 55 B.C. knew the British as a lead-producing people? There are mines reputed to be Roman or pre-Roman in Flintshire at Halkin and Dalar Goch; in Caernarfonshire above Betws-y-coed; in Montgomeryshire at Llanfyllin, Llangynog, Llanymynech, Pistyll Rhaeadr and Dylife; in Cardiganshire at Darren Fawr, Cwmsymlog and Cwmystwyth. And there are many others. But for nearly all of them the evidence of extreme antiquity is meagre. After all, how can you prove the ancientness of a mine whose earliest probings have almost always been obliterated by later workings? Then through all the 1,500 years down to Tudor times the records

of Welsh lead-mining remain exceedingly slender. We can only assume that the mines went fitfully on all that time, probably never on a great scale. We know that by Elizabeth Tudor's day, mining was at a very low ebb but was then stimulated by her creation of the Mines Royal Society, a corporation less interested in lead than in the silver that is found in many lead-mines. By the end of Elizabeth's reign, after the introduction of German technicians, Cardiganshire had contributed handsomely in silver to the London mint.

In the middle of James I's reign a famous gentleman took up residence near Aberystwyth. He was the Denbighshire-born engineer Sir Hugh Myddelton, an intimate friend of Raleigh.

The abandoned lead-mine at Cwmystwyth, Cardiganshire, one of several said to date back to prehistory.

Part of a leat which led water from a high reservoir down to a mine. These narrow, now dry, canals, sometimes several miles long, are still a typical feature of lead-mining country.

Both he and Raleigh were eager to find precious metals. Raleigh sought them down the Spanish Main. Myddelton came to Wales. He no doubt deserved the knighthood he had been given for bringing the New River to London in 1613, for it had left him almost penniless. But besides the knighthood he was also granted the right to make what he could out of the Mines Royal in Wales. So in 1617 he came to Cardiganshire, where he extracted silver from the lead ore at Cwmsymlog, Cwmystwyth and Tal-y-bont with immense success. From Cwmsymlog mine alone, for which he paid an annual rent of £400, his accounts showed him clearing £24,000 a year.

But it is typical of the ups and downs of lead-mining that after Myddelton's death the mines were allowed to drop into such immediate and thorough neglect that the next speculator, Thomas Bushell, who came only five years later, had virtually to begin all over again. But Bushell was an outstanding engineer. In half-a-dozen years, battling against disappointments galore, he had probed deeper into the rocks of Cardiganshire and overcome more mining problems than any man before him. He also revolutionised smelting methods, and his output of silver was so considerable that a mint was set up at Aberystwyth for the making of silver coins. Bushell heartily took up the Royalist cause in the

Civil War, and while making his own quick fortune had enough left over to give another fortune away to help the king. But the end of Charles's hopes at Naseby brought an abrupt finish to Bushell's nine years' reign over the ores of Cardiganshire. He became a fugitive from Cromwell, and most of his mines fell into disuse for the next half century.

One of the results of the decline in the power of the monarchy in late Stuart times was that the crown was forced to give up its old rights to all silver mines, leaving landowners free to exploit the precious ore in their own ground. Great days followed for mineral-rich Welsh estates: Powys, Lisburne, Gogerddan, Nant-eos and others. The mines began to attract heavy investment. One company, the Mine Adventurers, was floated with panache as 'the Welsh Potosi', because, if you believed the share-pushers' talk, this company was going to eclipse the fabulously-rich Bolivian silver mines after which it was named. Lewis Morris, writing in 1757, described Cardiganshire as the richest county that he knew. For many years after that the wealth continued to flow. But inevitably the drought set in at last, and by the early nineteenth century the mines were again in decay.

The next revival began from about the 1840s onwards. A new surge of enthusiasm, energy and capital associated with the arrival of the firm of Taylor and Sons inaugurated the age of modern mining in mid-Wales. Now Montgomeryshire as well as Cardiganshire received attention. Mines such as Craig y Mwyn at Llangynog, which had yielded well in the eighteenth century, were re-opened with astonishing success. Farther west at Van what was perhaps the richest Welsh vein of all time was struck, and for some years after 1870 Van mines became the centre of the wildest speculations. Said to have been sold for £42,000 in the 1860s, they were reckoned to be worth over £1 million by 1870.

But there came a disastrous slump in the price of lead about 1885, and very soon the industry in Wales was teetering on the edge of ruin. Though it was clung to here and there by those who could not believe that El Dorado was finished, it died quietly away in the early 1920s, and sporadic attempts at revival since have had little success.

And the future? As you wander about the Welsh hills and see how complete is the dereliction of the mines you may naturally suppose that here is the end of it all. But the same thing must often have been supposed in the past. In 1833, for instance, the topographer, Lewis, writes hopelessly of Cardiganshire: 'The lead mines have been abandoned for many years'. Yet it was only a few years later that a new fire of enthusiasm swept the industry and it was booming as never before. Today, though all seems so quiet and dead, there are miners and geologists who will tell you that much ore could still be found underground it if were sought deeply by modern methods. So are we destined one day, I wonder, to witness all the hopes and agonies of past centuries come circling round again?

(1962)

A SUBURBAN GREENSHANK

This was written in December, 1962, a time when the army was still using the Tonfannau area, near Tywyn, Merioneth, as a training ground.

A greenshank is normally among the wildest of our birds. Like most other waders he rises when you are still a quarter of a mile away. You get a brief look at his long, blackish, pointed wings that contrast with the brilliant whiteness of most of his body, and he probably calls a ringing *tew-tew-tew*. Then quickly he is gone, far down the estuary or across the marsh.

But recently at Tywyn in Merioneth, a greenshank took up residence—yes, that just describes it—in the heart of a human community. He appeared one morning on someone's front lawn in the army's married quarters estate just behind the coast on the north side of the town. This is a small, modern housing estate, differing from

A greenshank which frequented suburban lawns at Tywyn, Meirionnydd, in November-December, 1962.

other housing estates in only one particular but an important one: instead of having front gardens, the houses have closely cut lawns. Even so, it is decidedly not greenshank habitat. For greenshanks, especially our greenshanks of the autumn and winter estuary pick their food out of shallow water and mud—presumably shrimps, shellfish and other marine creatures.

Right from the start this Tywyn greenshank was different. Although saltings and mudflats stretch widely a mile north, he remained all day and every day on the lawns of the housing estate—his one food being earthworms, earthworms, earthworms. These he found very expertly: even in the hoar frost of early morning he could pull them out, swallowing them one after another, choosing as far as I could see only worms that were several inches long. Then there was his tameness. This was most extraordinary. Cars passed frequently, dogs barked, children played. There were bakers and butchers, workmen and shopping women. From windows came the noise of wireless sets, vacuum cleaners and all sorts of clatter.

Photographers stalked him. Infants almost touched him. Groups of adults stood and watched him. It made no difference: he had joined the community and there he would stay. If you were gentle in your approach, he would allow you to within three yards. If you were ungentle, as the toddlers and the cats sometimes were, he simply rose and flew over the houses to someone else's lawn.

He quickly became well known. Residents who did not know what he was and had never been interested in a bird before became quite fascinated by this greenshank. If you appeared with binoculars someone would soon ask you: 'Are you looking for the bird? He was outside No. 14 five minutes ago'. And if you couldn't find him at No. 14 you would soon find someone who knew where he was.

He came about the middle of November and he kept up this strange manner of life for about three weeks. Then his enthusiasm for suburbia evidently waned, for one day he was noted as flying away to the mudflats. (You see how little private life he had.) And though he came back to the lawns a few days later, he was clearly getting less addicted to earthworms and well-manicured lawns. Soon his visits ceased altogether.

Presumably even he had felt the pull of migration at last and had followed his fellow greenshanks to Africa. I still treasure the memory of his sojourn at Tywyn. At a time when we hear so much about vandalism and cruelty, I like to think of the protective interest this trusting bird aroused in a whole community of people.

(1962)

Part of the housing estate at Tywyn where the eccentric greenshank stayed for several weeks in 1962.

SWALLOW DAYS

Swallows may be no more joyous than other birds, but they seem so full of life and song, and such lovers of sunlight, breezes and blue skies that we habitually link them with the happier side of existence. Not that even they are free from duller moments. I have gone round the cowsheds on cold wet mornings and seen all our swallows sitting along the beams waiting for the rain to stop, and there they have remained for hours looking quite dejected, as if wondering why they ever left the sun and warmth of Africa. But eventually the rain eases, their spirits revive and off they go, flickering low across the fields to hunt flies in the lee of the woods.

They can be delightfully confiding when they first come in spring and are looking for nest sites. As there is not room for them all in the cowsheds—each pair of swallows requires a lot of space—they investigate our house as well. Sometimes on April mornings just after dawn we are wakened by a pair flying in through the bedroom window to perch twittering on a mirror or a cupboard. Then down in the kitchen at breakfast-time, if we leave the door open, a swallow will occasionally come shooting in, flutter round the room and go arrowing out again, giving us a wonderful blue gleam as his wings take the sunlight.

Last year a pair would have nested in our bedroom if we had allowed them. For a week they flew in and out all day and roosted with us at night, one at each end of the curtain rod. We got to know them well and they us. Seeing us switch on the light and getting into bed never worried them. They had their fixed places and times: always the male at the same end of the curtain, the female at the other. Always the male woke first, sang and then went out. The female woke half to three-quarters of an hour later than he, often not until he brought her a beakful of flies, which were accepted amid courtship excitement.

Alas, our bedroom window opens to the south-west and often has to be closed to keep out the floods of rain that blow in from the Atlantic. Very reluctantly we shut our swallows out. But though they were banished from the house, there were still the stable, the potting shed and the outside lavatory, which in Wales we call the Tŷ Bach (little house). All these the pair inspected thoroughly, and then they opted for the potting shed. In a few days they built a nest on a box hanging on one of the walls, and between spells of building they sat near each other on the wires while the cock sang with wide-open mouth.

But soon there was trouble. A new pair of swallows arrived and swooped aggressively in and out of the potting shed. Days of the intensest rivalry followed. Yet there was no vulgar sparrow-like squabbling. Instead, there were long discussions on the wires until terms for peaceful co-existence were agreed on. But this upset had been enough to break the first pair's breeding rhythm, and the nest on the box was abandoned. So was the potting shed: clearly it had been settled that since there was not enough room for both pairs in there, neither should have it. That still left the stable and the Tŷ Bach, and eventually we had a nest in each.

The swallows' access to the Tŷ Bach was through a space 4 inches wide above the door. It was wonderful to see them come curving sharply round the corner of the building and go swooping in through that narrow space with no apparent loss of speed. Having already got to know us in the bedroom, they were very tame. Daily we watched them bringing wet muck from outside the cowshed and sticking it on to the wall. Or they flew to the garden and picked up dried grasses and dipped them in mud and so made bricks in the way that early man made bricks. Then came feathers for the lining; and soon there were eggs in the nest and then young. When the newly white-washed wall began to be

A swallow's nest in the *tŷ bach* (outside lavatory) at Ynys Edwin.

spattered we hung a sheet of brown paper to protect it. Every day the swallows brought more and more insects and now and then I examined the floor below for food which the birds accidentally dropped and I was grateful to find the blood-sucking horse-flies frequent among their victims.

While the Tŷ Bach pair thrived, the nest in the stable had no luck at all. When the female had laid one egg something went wrong. Presumably she became egg-bound, for she laid no more. For four days she perched moping on a beam by the nest. Then she began to incubate her one egg, but in a few days deserted it.

The spring days passed. One after another, around midsummer, the several swallow broods in the cowshed and then the one in the Tŷ Bach took to the wing. More and more nests lay deserted while the outside air and the telephone wires grew daily more murmurous with young swallows. But though they joined up in one flock by day, yet each night for nearly a fortnight all the young returned to their own nests.

Then the parents mated again, and once more there were eggs in many of the nests and the young slept in little huddles on the beams. For several more days they were fed by the cock birds while the females incubated. But quickly the young learned to get their own food, and by the time the second broods were flying, many young of the first broods had gone.

Some had wandered away to swell the August flocks. But many were taken by a pair of sparrowhawks that came several times a day from the wood across the lambing field, for the hawks had a large brood to feed. It was sad to see the young swallows going like this. But nearly every year it is the same. That is how life is, and we must accept it as the swallows do. The hawk comes; there is panic, anger, death; and a few minutes later the incident is forgotten and there is only the twittering, the gaiety and the sunlight.

(1964)

ROADS TO AN ANCIENT LAND

It was on a November day of bright sun and showers that I climbed steeply from the village of Bont-ddu on the Mawddach estuary in Merioneth, up through woods bright with the yellow of hazels and the deep bronze of oak and beech, up onto the open mountains, past the last inhabited farm and on along the mountain road that leads you towards the sea in the north-west. Not that I could see the sea yet. Nor would I until I reached the top of the next far ridge. And I now saw that I had to go down into a wide upland valley before I could begin to climb again. I looked about me. Everywhere stretched bracken, gorse and dry stone walls. The sun gleamed on rocks wet by the last splutter of rain. A sheep stared at me, gave a sneeze of alarm and clattered away over loose stones and I was alone in the silence of the hills.

I looked back for the last time at the Mawddach. The tide was streaming seawards leaving ribbons of black water between silvery sandbanks. Beyond the estuary I looked at the long high ridge of Cader Idris, the east end veiled by grey sweeping rain, the western half lit by the sun. Then I turned and took to the road again. It was a green road that I followed. Green, that is, where it was not smooth bare rock. And green roads, I thought as I went along between stone walls, should be kept always green for there are few of them left nowadays. They have, in fact, become something precious, something to be guarded from that tourism-mad individual who seems to sit on every Welsh county council demanding that every mountain road be made motorable and so turned into a tourist attraction.

Not that there seemed much danger of this dipping, clambering, twisting track ever being made up. I was only a mile or two along it and already it was hinting at failure. Where drains had blocked and streams had come over instead of under, it disappeared under mud and rushes or had been gouged deeply by floods. The wonder was that wheels had ever negotiated it as they must have done and as recently as 1820. For until then, though all appearances now ridicule the idea, this was the main road, the only road for vehicles bound from Dolgellau via Bont-ddu to Harlech. In 1820 the present road was cut along the estuary to take in Barmouth. Before then you jerked and jostled your way up and over this mountain track, along which a milestone or two still speak of its former importance.

I went on down the slope. And as I got further amongst the hills I might have lost the road altogether were its course not marked onward by the faithful walls alongside. Then when the walls at last gave out I steered by dead reckoning through bracken and gorse till I dipped to a stream and found the road again where it is still carefully bridged with large slabs and supporting boulders no flood has yet disturbed.

The rampart of hills was now close before me, for the road and I had now reached the middle of this wide and empty valley far out in the tawny autumn moorlands. I looked at the barrier ahead and wondered how the road would find a way. I passed a small standing stone beside the track and wondered at its lonely purpose out there on the moor. Slowly I crossed the lowest, wettest part of the valley and reached the foot of the slope. Here the road has to decide and quite abruptly it does so. Quite abruptly it turns and takes to the hillside and immediately you are out of rushes and mud and are back on the springing hill turf with dead bracken all about you rustling in the wind. And you note with gladness that the guiding wall is with you again; for if on your way back you get benighted (as I did) then that wall will be your comfort and your friend. But though the road climbs it does so only slantingly, edging always leftwards, seawards, until with despair you see it is threatening to go all the way round the end of the spur instead of making a short steep canter over the top. But then comes the surprise. Quite suddenly it is as if the road decides the leg-pull has gone far enough. It leaves its wall and all guiding marks and strides away straight up the hillside making for a shallow saddle 500 very steep feet above. (Surely they needed extra horses for that bit?) As a winding hollow way in the turf it climbs up to a gate in a wall that crowns the ridge. With a thought for the straining horses of olden time you bend your back, brace your legs and plod up to the gap. You have reached the road's highest point, the pass called Bwlch y Rhiwgyr—an informative name to find along a road for it suggests a drovers' pass. Here, dramatically held in the V of a narrow defile, a wild and uninhabited plain is before you, and all north Cardigan Bay and the splendid mountains of Llŷn stand round the horizon.

Quickly the road drops you to this plain, this wide shelf that stands about 1,000 feet above the sea and looks down at the distant white waves breaking along ten miles of sandy shore. It is poor, very poor ground agriculturally, this desolate plateau scattered with rocks from broken hillsides and with bogs and rushes everywhere. Further north behind Harlech this shelf is kinder and supports a scatter of delightful little farms. But here nearer to the Mawddach the soil is far less hospitable. A few derelict houses mark a century old tide-mark of human settlement long receded and there is now no occupied house along the road till you come down to Corsygedol, a fine Elizabethan mansion whose history is closely linked with the history of this ancient road.

But though modern man has abandoned the plateau, primitive man used it with enthusiasm, perhaps at a time when the climate was kinder. For scattered over it even now are relics of his life there and of his death. There are, for instance, the cairns. Several of these are visible from the road but none nearly so impressive as the pair known as Carneddau Hengwm. They

Bwlch y Rhiwgyr ('Drovers' Pass') is the highest point on the ancient road from Bont-ddu over the hills towards Harlech. The view is from the north-west.

A chambered tomb in the Neolithic cairns of Carneddau Hengwm near Barmouth.

Pen y Dinas, an Iron Age hill-fort three miles north of Barmouth.

must, I think, be about the biggest cairns in Wales, or, at any rate, have been. Not that they are built high so much as long, one of them 150 feet long in fact. They form two parallel heaps of loose rocks with at least one chambered tomb in each. If ever these were covered with earth they were huge barrows indeed; for what is left is almost certainly only a fragment of what was there before the despoilers of past centuries got at these fine cairns and carted their rocks off wholesale to build field walls.

So we can speak of all the ancient relics of this plateau: perhaps only a tithe remains of all that once stood thereabouts. It is possible, I suppose, that the cairns, stone-circles, standing stones and hut-circles were preserved through a great stretch of the civilised period simply because they were held in dread and superstition. But modern man has treated them with contempt, has made use of them or ignorantly thrown them aside.

No matter what he has done to the cromlechs and the cairns, man has not been able to destroy the Iron Age hill-forts. Their characteristic outlines are still clearly cut out against the sky. You see the first as soon as you come up the hill from Bont-ddu; the second is Pen y Dinas close to Carneddau Hengwm; the third and best is Craig y Dinas towering over the moorland stream they call Ysgethin. Craig y Dinas is an exception among hill-camps. Normally their rings are of earth only, or a mixture of earth and rock. But this sharp hill of Craig y Dinas is topped by considerable walls of stone or rather the collapsed wreck of considerable walls. There they lie where they fell maybe 2000 years ago.

From Craig y Dinas I looked back along the way I had come. From up there I could see more clearly than ever the wild nature of that bit of country. I looked across miles of rock-scattered moorland criss-crossed by the straight lines of walls. One large 'field' was a complete waste of rocks, a deep grey sea of rocks (glacier-sown?) with cavities and caves going down between them into unknown depths and forming refuges spacious enough to hide all the hill-foxes, polecats and pine martens in Britain. Having scrambled down from Craig y Dinas I clambered

Pont Scethin, a bridge on the eighteenth-century road from Dolgellau to Harlech via Bont-ddu.

The old road approaching Pont Scethin from Bont-ddu.

across this extraordinary boulder field with difficulty, thankful to reach smooth turf at last and make my way to the edge of a black lake that lies under blacker cliffs. This is the lake called Irddyn, one of the many fabled lakes of the Celtic world. At its edge are several bewildering accumulations of rock debris in which you may or may not see the remains of ancient structures: but at least there is the tradition of an ancient settlement there.

So much for the ruined habitations and the despoiled burials of our or somebody's ancestors. I daresay time and the weather have been the chief wreckers of the dwellings, the hill-forts, the many hut-circles. But it is man who has pillaged the tombs, mostly man of the eighteenth and nineteenth centuries, often carelessly destroying what he unearthed and recording little with accuracy. I hope the age of opening such cairns is now over. For surely enough is now known of their probable contents? And is there anything more deflating than to discover an opened cairn, a pile of stones with, in the centre, not a peak but a hollow, and in the hollow an empty grave?

That day I had intended to walk on to Harlech along the ancient road that crosses the Ysgethin at Pont Scethin; but now here I was still at the edge of Llyn Irddyn, much less than half-way there and the day nearly spent. Nor had I gone up Moelfre, the shapely hill behind Craig y Dinas. On Moelfre, too, I remembered from a visit years ago, I would have found traces of man's far past. But I was more than content to have seen a part of this land so rich in ancient things, this plateau that is a slice of prehistoric Britain miraculously surviving. I returned along the road towards Bont-ddu. On top of Bwlch y Rhiwgyr I rested a moment and looked back across the plateau. The wind grew cold as a grey wall of rain came up Cardigan Bay towards Snowdon. The hills darkened all round. Then unexpectedly against the black flank of Moelfre the walls on Craig y Dinas caught a momentary gleam of sunlight. I thought of the men who a couple of thousand years ago had toiled up those steep banks with all those tons of rock and had built them carefully into walls over 15 feet thick. Then, as I watched, rain swallowed everything.

(1964)

87

MEDIEVAL NATURE RESERVES

Does anything made by man endure like a bank of earth? Castles come and castles go but turf-covered banks, if they do not last for ever, are certainly good for two or three thousand years. So it is not surprising that the earthworks of every age of man still stand up in great numbers in the countryside. Even in this county, Cardiganshire, which is not famous for antiquities, there are something like 120 hill-forts and castle-mounds besides numerous dikes and ditches and tumuli. Many of them, left undisturbed either out of superstition or reverence, or because they were awkward to plough or remove, have survived into our day as unintentional little nature reserves.

I have had many a happy day seeking out the castle-mounds of Cardiganshire, the mottes and baileys built in or about the twelfth and thirteenth centuries, some by the Welsh, some by the Norman chieftains who carved up Wales and each other with bewildering frequency. These mottes are usually tucked comfortably away in the valleys, in delectable sites by streams or rivers, and built of good soils that grow a variety of plants as well as thickets to hide foxes, badgers and birds.

It was mid-May when I last did the round of our local mottes and I soon discovered that mottes and bluebells are inseparable. Obviously bluebells like the deep soil and perfect drainage they find there; and a motte at Trefilan near the Aeron valley, a perfectly preserved castle-mound and ditch overgrown with sycamores, was a solid dome of bluebells. Near by gurgled the stream that had supplied water for the moat, rooks cawed near the church, willow warblers sang in the leafing sycamores: the year was at its best. What did it matter that all we seem to know of the history of the castle of Trefilan is that it was repaired in 1233 by Maelgwn Fychan ap Maelgwn ap Rhys?

I was more interested to speculate how long it took, after the castle decayed, for the bluebells, the sycamores and the willow warblers to take over. I imagined the mound standing bleak and bare, its crowning wooden palisade gradually rotting and sagging into the moat; and the moat itself filling and drying. Nettles would come, and docks, dandelions, groundsels, plantains. But no trees yet. For those were goat-cursed days and all seedling trees would have been eaten. I doubt the bluebells too—because of the pigs. The effect of pigs came home to me when I got to the motte of old Aberystwyth castle, which tops a hill with splendid ocean views a mile south of the town. There great patches of the turf on the earthworks had been ravaged by pigs digging for bluebell bulbs. If that could happen in these days when free-range pigs are few, what hope for the bluebells of the Middle Ages, when pigs were legion and lived almost entirely off the land? So I envisage the disused mottes standing up treeless and flowerless for maybe several centuries, and guess that it is much nearer our own time that they acquired those concealing thickets.

The site of Humphrey's Castle near the Teifi valley in south Cardiganshire. Many medieval castle-mounds have become unintentional nature reserves.

Lanceolate spleenwort (*Asplenium lanceolatum*). Sometimes called 'the Barmouth fern' by Victorian fern-collectors, it is an uncommon species of coastal districts in west Wales.

40 yards before my mind caught up with my eye. I stopped. Surely there had been something a little different about that fern? I felt compelled to go back and bend and examine. And there it was, one, no two, no, a whole row of glossy green plants of the fern I had sought that morning. I went home rejoicing that after a century and a quarter we can still say with Emilius Nicholson: 'In this vicinity are found *Asplenium lanceolatum*'.

(1965)

FLOWERS IN THE SEA WINDS

The Great Orme on the north coast of Wales can be an enormous surprise if you are not prepared for it. Coming up through Merioneth and Caernarfonshire you travel for many miles through rocks that are dark all the way. You are practically in Llandudno, almost at the end of the land, when suddenly the brilliant white shape of the Orme breaks upon your astonished gaze. Faced by these pale, bare terraces of limestone you have a momentary illusion that you have come to Ingleborough or Teesdale, or rather, seeing the blue sea beyond, you may think of the cliffs of the Burren in western Ireland.

But though the Great Orme stands alone, dipping its skirts into the sea on three sides, it is not, geologically speaking, as isolated as it looks. It is in fact part of a belt of Carboniferous Limestone that begins in the west in Anglesey and crops up intermittently at the Great and Little Ormes and various hills across north Wales, finally bending south in a splendid arc to finish at Llanymynech on the Shropshire border. All the way its course is marked onward by one good botanical site after another where you can see lime-loving species rare elsewhere on the predominantly acid soils of Wales.

It is the Great Orme that is botanically the best-known of all the north Wales limestone. The name, by the way, is neither Welsh nor English but Viking. However, if the Vikings once had it and the Welsh have it now, you could be forgiven, if led there blindfolded, for supposing when you heard the speech that is dominant on any summer's day, that you were in a public park somewhere in England. For this magnificent open space set high above the sea is the holiday playground of thousands who come every year from beyond Offa's Dyke. On any fine day you will find cars parked, picnics spread out and crowds of scavenging gulls.

Not, on the face of it, the most promising spot for a plant-seeker. But by a happy accident the Great Orme's best plants and the Great Orme's hordes of people are by nature separated. The habitat of the people is the level or only gently sloping turf of the top of the Orme. Most of the choicer plants are where rocks make walking uncomfortable or down slopes dense with scrub or on sheer cliffs. And those species which do get trodden on—squills, spring cinquefoil, hoary rock-rose—are well past their best before the real summer crowds start to gather.

You need to make several trips to the Orme between spring and autumn if you are to see the whole range of its flora. It is best to go as early as April or even March to catch the tiny white flowers of that soon-fading little crucifer, hutchinsia or rock pepperwort. And go not later than May (even though the books say June) to be sure of finding the yellow flowers of the spring cinquefoil. Besides, even if they persist into June, they are not easy to find among the welter of rock-roses which by then have come into bloom.

Rock-roses are of two kinds on the Orme, both in the greatest plenty. First comes the hoary rock-rose in May. When you see the opulence with which this endearing little species has spread its yellow flowers from end to end of the Orme you marvel that it should not be equally happy in many other limestone areas. Yet apart from a few other localities in Wales and north-west England and a very restricted area in western Ireland the hoary rock-rose is absent from most of the botanically classic limestone areas of the British Isles. Compared with other rock-roses its flowering time is brief. On the Orme it is usually all over by the first week of July, leaving the larger-flowered common rock-rose to go on till the autumn.

Vernal squill, spring sandwort, horseshoe vetch: all three you may find lingering on the Orme till July; but only just. The squill is at its blue-carpet best in April-May; in May, too, the

Southampton
High **26** | Low **16**
Precipitation: 45%
Showers

Aberdeen
High **20** | Low **11**
Precipitation: 5%
Sunny spells

Glasgow
High **19** | Low **10**
Precipitation: 0%
Sunny spells

Cardiff
High **21** | Low **14**
Precipitation: 20%
Sunny spells

Belfast
High **19** | Low **11**
Precipitation: 5%
Sunny spells

Weather view

Sunset and moonrise over the Great Orme, Llandudno, Wales, seen from a small boat Photograph: Derek Taylor/ GuardianWitness

Share your pictures of this week's weather at theguardian. com/ weather-view

guardian witness

powered by EE

Liberal

But not

with th

Foliage of the Great Orme's wild cotoneaster.

sandwort opens most of its white stars; the dainty yellow flowers of the vetch are finest in May or June, though its curiously shaped seed-pods are worth looking for in July. A good May to mid-July Orme plant, tall and delicate-looking, is the Nottingham catchfly, whose long white petals are usually kept tightly rolled up during the daytime leading you to think they are over. But examine them again towards evening, and you will find them unfurling again. For it is in the warm summer darkness that this plant sheds its fragrance to attract the moths.

On the Orme this catchfly has much more showy neighbours. The blood-red cranesbill spreads beauty in all directions. There are several rare hawkweeds pursued only by dedicated botanists. And there is the spotted cat's-ear which is a princess among the Compositae, having both outstanding rarity and beauty. From a basal rosette of broad, dark-green, purple-spotted, attractively hairy leaves there rises a tall, almost leafless stem topped by a splendid mop of a flower, deeply yellow and measuring nearly 2 inches across.

As for the Great Orme's most noteworthy plant, *Cotoneaster integerrimus*, the wild cotoneaster, which grows here and nowhere else in the British Isles, it is not easy to assess its fortunes. But the general belief seems to be that

it is now rarer on the Orme than when it was first discovered in 1783. It is even more difficult to say how it got there in the beginning. I suppose we can talk about relict floras and argue that this cotoneaster must have been wider-spread in Britain formerly. But I find it easier to imagine

Dark-red helleborine, an uncommon orchid of the Great Orme, Llandudno.

an October fieldfare arriving on the Orme and leaving on some ledge a dropping containing seeds that were in a berry the bird had swallowed in the mountains of Scandinavia the previous day.

This cotoneaster is distinctive. Its leaves are full and roundish, a dull matt-green and deciduous: and therefore not confusable with the little, glossy, evergreen leaves of the vastly commoner *Cotoneaster microphyllus*, which is a formidable spreader and a successful escaper from gardens. On the Orme it enjoys rampaging across the territory of the rare catchflies and cat's-ears and has to be restrained.

Come July, and the Orme's later flowers are beginning to show. The lovely spiked speedwell is thrusting its slender blue spires through the surrounding herbage and will continue to do so till September. On the driest rocks, very sparingly, the dark-red helleborine comes into bloom where the teeth of sheep cannot reach it. Then in September and lasting into October, a final rarity: goldilocks, a yellow-headed, linear-leaved, delicate composite known only on a few other limestone headlands of western Britain.

But whether you botanise on the Orme in spring or in autumn you will always find it a very interesting, even remarkable, place. You can spend hours scrambling about steep, shrubby and rocky thickets with the roar of the town immediately below. You may or may not see the rarities you seek, but you will certainly find a fascinating struggle going on between the native species and a real hugger-mugger of escapes and throw-outs—anything from Turkey oaks and exotic pines to red valerian and snapdragons. And when you have sweated enough on that south-facing slope you can withdraw to cooler heights on the cliffs where you can enjoy far views of coast and ocean. With the yellow spires of wild cabbage flowers all about you and the voices of fulmars, gulls and kittiwakes on the air, you might be on the wildest cliff of Britain instead of in a popular town park.

(1969)

Cliffs of the Great Orme, Llandudno.

96

glories of that park was a rare collection of medieval inscribed stones. I was not disappointed: those relics with their simple messages from the Middle Ages I found more moving than many a vast cathedral. Then exploring further to look for fallow deer in the ancient park I wandered up to the highest ground and there I found a hill-fort, Mynydd Castell, seven acres at a guess, enclosed within a single circular bank. I know I could have sought out more spectacular, multiple-banked hill-forts not far distant but at Mynydd Castell I got a unique perspective on local history: from the quiet, grassy ramparts of the Celtic Iron Age I looked down on the Iron Age of today—the vast sprawl of the Margam Abbey steelworks.

For a contrast with industry I went to Llanmadog at the western end of Gower. On what is almost the highest point of that fair peninsula is a nobly sited hill-fort called the Bulwark from which I looked back across nearly the whole of Gower. The northward view was equally heart-lifting across the wide dunes and marshes of Whitford Burrows and away across the Loughor estuary to more dunes and saltings along the coast of Carmarthenshire.

If you will allow two hill-forts side by side to count as one, then I would guess that the most extensive in Wales must be Carn Goch in Carmarthenshire. It is on a hill near Bethlehem, five miles up the Tywi from Llandeilo. Biggest or not, Carn Goch is certainly worth a visit to see its great though crumpled walls which still reach twenty feet in places and have a total length of several miles. A rather wonderful place. If I had to name my second favourite hill-fort after Tre'r Ceiri I am sure it would be this huge, evocative citadel of Carn Goch.

Up in north Carmarthenshire I found Vortigern's hill-fort, the only one I know that is linked by name with someone who managed, however briefly, to edge his way onto the margins of history, as distinct from even more shadowy figures like Arthur whose story seems to lie deep in the realm of legend. Vortigern (in Welsh, Gwrtheyrn) was king of southern Britain in the fifth century. His hill-fort, Craig Gwrtheyrn, tops a steep wooded hill above the River Teifi, a mile east of Llandysul. Vortigern is dismally remembered by history for inviting the Saxons into England to help against the invading Picts. Afterwards, as we all know, the Saxons declined to go home. Disgraced by this incident (here legend takes up the story) Vortigern is supposed to have come into Wales and found refuge at Craig Gwrtheyrn. This unlikely tale is no doubt an invention of those prolific medieval story-tellers who delighted in explaining place-names by ingenious fables. To add to the doubt scholars have pointed out that Vortigern was not an uncommon name and that this hill-fort could commemorate someone else entirely.

I ended my hill-fort odyssey in Pembroke-shire: but out of all its wealth of earthworks two must suffice. First I went to a muscular outlier of the Presely Hills, Carn Ingli, because the map told me I would find hut-circles as well as a hill-fort up there. Wild, rock-strewn and heathery, Carn Ingli came up to all my expectations, its strong defences and hut remains putting me in mind, as at Caer Drewyn, of Caernarfonshire's Tre'r Ceiri. Its ramparts, I discovered, were different from any I had seen elsewhere: they filled gaps between scattered crags, joining them to form an obstacle to all invaders. But even had I found no hill-fort, no hut-circles up there, the prospect of Newport and its bay and the great sea-washed headlands of Strumble, Dinas and Cemais would have made the walk one to be remembered always.

My last hill-fort was the farthest west. A gale off the Atlantic, threatening rain, roared in my ears as I walked or stumbled past the Neolithic burial chamber, Coetan Arthur, on my way to St. David's Head. I was glad to crouch out of the wind under the bank of earth and stones which the Iron Age people built across the headland to create their strong promontory fort. With difficulty in that near-hurricane I made my way past a group of hut-circles up to the highest rocks. I watched the tormented sea and the waves crashing in whiteness up the cliffs. And I thought of those who lived there through the storms of how many forgotten years? Then the day darkened into deluges of lashing rain and furious squalls. So from the Iron Age of prehistory I retreated in haste down the hill to my car and the Iron Age of the twentieth century.

(1970)

The Teifi river just upstream from Pontrhydfendigaid, Cardiganshire. The distant hill, Pen y Bannau, is crowned by an Iron Age fort.

WHERE HAVE ALL THE WOODLARKS GONE?

I wrote this threnody in 1973. Alas, we still look in vain for the woodlarks' return.

There was a time (but it is years ago now) when I seriously thought I would write a book about the woodlark. For in those days this was a bird I met with nearly every time I went out of doors and the more I heard and saw of it, the more interested I became. I first heard a woodlark in my youth one sparkling April day on the Clent Hills in Worcestershire. I thought it the finest song I had ever listened to; and though I have heard many other birds since then, it is still the song of the woodlark that delights me most.

In the Midlands woodlarks were scarce, and I had no chance of getting at all familiar with them until years later when I married and came to live in Wales. My wife and I lived for a time in a little upland cottage close to Plynlimon where, at 1,000 ft, the woodlark's song came to us across rushy moorland along with the bleating of snipe and the yodelling of curlews. But at that altitude woodlarks were uncommon and it was not till we moved down to a village near the sea that we found them everywhere, all over the coastal hills and valleys right out to the breezy cliffs.

In the spring we often discovered their nests, but only after patient watching. Most we found hidden in bracken on the slopes, though some were in fields of young corn and occasionally, as befits a bird with such a name, the nests were in woods. Never large woods, only small copses and thickets. The woodlarks were very often near houses. There were plenty of them, for instance, on the outskirts of Aberystwyth where I often heard them in the grounds of the National Library. The most suburban nest-site I saw, as well as the most remarkable, was in a shallow box containing experimental grass, one of many similar boxes placed on the ground in rows close to greenhouses of the College Botanic Garden, with people passing to and fro all day. The wonder was not only that a 'field' 2 ft by 1 ft was a sufficient nesting place but that the birds could also remember which was their box among so many exactly the same size and shape.

March was the woodlarks' great month. Day after day I went out on clear frosty mornings to watch and listen. I had only to go through a gate at the end of our garden, climb the nearby hill and there I was alone in the still and frigid air with the woodlarks singing, chasing, mating and building their nests. I wrote everything down and my notebooks grew fat. But those were restless days, and soon we moved, this time northwards. Not many miles but it meant a change of county by crossing the Dyfi estuary to Merioneth. To a woodlark enthusiast this looked a depressing move because the *Handbook of British Birds* (first edition) was quite uncompromising on the breeding distribution of the woodlark in Wales: 'Not in Merioneth', it said. As definite as that.

A woodlark nesting in a field of oats in Cardiganshire in the spring of 1960. The severe winter of 1962-3 virtually exterminated the woodlark here.

A woodlark's nest on a brackeny hillside, the commonest habitat for woodlarks when they were abundant in south and central Wales.

(Harold Wright)

our little cottage and garden seemed to serve as a focus for all the activities of this woodlark community. When I should have been at other tasks I spent long hours adding more and more notes on their courtship, their squabbling, their nests, eggs and young. Their lives filled my days as their songs filled my ears. I now look back on that spring with the woodlarks on a beautiful Merioneth hill as a real idyll; and one never to be repeated, for again we moved—back south across the shining estuary to Cardiganshire.

The years passed. But the woodlarks never lost their delight for us. My hopes of writing a book about them remained. I sketched out its main topics: the woodlark's world distribution, for example: how it was almost purely a bird of Europe. And how its place in Britain was decidedly in the south, suggesting a species that was only half-hardy. Other chapters were planned, and meanwhile I went on making notes, taking photographs. I felt in no hurry. The woodlarks would always be there and the longer I studied them the more I would learn.

I had reckoned without the accidents of nature, the ups and downs of birds' fortunes, those cycles of widening and shrinking that we would find affecting the numbers of all species of animals and plants if only our records could go back far enough. The winter of 1962-3 arrived, one of the very coldest and snowiest, when birds died in multitudes. Among the resident species in our district those that suffered most included long-tailed tit, mistle thrush, wren, kingfisher, green woodpecker, barn owl—and woodlark.

It was a sad spring that followed, with so many favourite birds quite absent or rare. But we had no long-term worries. We had lived through other such bad spells and felt confident that, as before, even the most affected birds would recover in a few seasons. And so it proved for all of them except one—the woodlark. After four years, by which time the other species were getting back to normal, I had neither seen nor heard a woodlark. Then in the fifth year—

But the *Handbook* had been written in 1938 and our move to Merioneth was twelve years later. By which time the woodlark had also moved north and put the *Handbook* out of date.

So it was that, around our cottage on the hills above Aberdyfi, we had more woodlarks than ever before. Or rather they were closer. What a joy it was to find them as a garden bird. They sang above us all day, either circling in the air or standing on the roof. We were completely isolated, above oakwoods that dropped steeply to the estuary: all round us was bracken, gorse, grass and rock—perfect woodlark country. And delicious moment—I did hear one. There it was, the old cheerful tune carolling down from the sky. The woodlark, it seemed, was going to make a come back after all.

Not so. That solitary singer was there for one spring, then another, then no more. And now ten years have passed since the great frost, and the woodlark has virtually disappeared not merely from this part of Cardiganshire but is described as hard to find in many of its former habitats in southern England and Wales. Like wryneck and red-backed shrike it is retreating to the Continent. And who can prophesy when it will return?

But why should the woodlark have gone like this and so suddenly? Was the winter of 1962-3 so much more terrible than previous arctic spells? What about 1947 for instance? That year brought dreadful weather from late January to March, yet the woodlark survived. So perhaps the truth is, as some observers claim, that the woodlark was already declining in many districts and that the 1962-3 winter merely pushed it further down the slope.

So I bid the woodlark farewell. My diaries lie gathering the dust and my book will never be written, which I daresay will be no loss to the world, only a source of regret to me when I think how I would have enjoyed writing in praise of so admirable a bird. To me the countryside would be poorer for the loss of any kind of bird, even crow, starling or sparrow. But, to have lost the woodlark of all birds, is melancholy indeed.

(1973)

Greenhouses at the College Botany Gardens, Aberystwyth. There was a woodlark's nest in one of the boxes in the foreground in spring, c. 1960.

An experimental grass plant in which woodlarks nested.

MARTS SWEET AND FOUL

In almost any parish in Wales, if you plod your way through the churchwardens' accounts of the eighteenth or early nineteenth centuries, you will find, amid a mass of badly spelt English and Welsh, reference after reference to monies paid out for the destruction of unpopular animals. 'To Dai Jones pd. fourpence for kill fulbart' (a polecat). 'To Evans, miller, 3s 6d. for cild old fockis Bitcht and four Youngers.' *'Am ladd cath goed* [For killing a wood cat] 3s. 4d.' So they go remorsely on, these chronicles of endless war between man and hostile nature.

A wonderful source, you might suppose, these parochial archives, for the history of our wild fauna. But you would be only partly correct. The truth is that there are hideous difficulties of interpretation, especially because two languages are involved. Take the wild cat. In the records it may be explicitly 'wild cat' or *'cath wyllt'*. But more often it is just 'cat' or *'cath'*. Occasionally it is 'mountain cat' or *'cath fynydd'*. Very often it is 'wood cat' or *'cath goed'*. All quite satisfactory until we realise that any of these names were also used locally for martens, polecats and heaven knows what else. Do not forget that 'puss' was in common use for a hare. So was *'cath eithin'* (a 'furze cat'). This complete universality of 'cat' stems from the fact that in one form or another it has existed since ancient times in Greek, Latin, Celtic, Teutonic and Slavonic languages and in its long history has been applied to many different animals.

So archivists have to accept that 'wild cat' and all its variants in the old records are rather useless words leaving us for ever more in doubt about how long *Felis sylvestris*, the true wild cat, went on surviving in Wales. What would help would be a good range of dated and genuinely Welsh wild cat specimens in museums. But these are lacking: and all is speculation and assumption.

It is safer to talk about pine martens (formerly 'marten cats'). At least we have genuine Welsh specimens preserved and the language has a better word than merely *cath*. It is *bele* (pronounced something like 'bellay') and when the parish scribes wrote *bele* there is no doubt they often meant a marten. Other Welsh words for marten are less reliable, *carlwm*, for instance. Of my two Welsh dictionaries one defines *carlwm* as a marten, the other says it is a stoat. J. Walters's dictionary of 1794 even tells us that a marten is *'rhyw wiwair'* which means 'a sort of squirrel'!

Despite the problems of semantics we can be sure that martens were fairly common in Wales until towards the end of last century. They were an accepted, if unwelcome, part of everyday rural life in many districts, and even an object of the chase. Yet in our century, which has on the whole favoured the survival of predators in Wales, the marten has become exceedingly rare. This is especially strange when you compare its fortunes with those of its relative, the *ffwlbart* or polecat. By the end of last century these two seem to have been about equally uncommon here. But since then the marten (or sweetmart) has gone further downhill while the polecat (or foulmart) has prospered almost beyond belief.

It has all happened since World War I. Till then the Welsh gamekeepers kept the ranks of martens and polecats very thin indeed. Then after 1914 gamekeeping virtually ceased and in many districts was never resumed after 1918 on anything like the pre-war scale. Most predators were soon thriving abundantly. But not the pine marten. Why? There is or used to be a theory that once a species is reduced to a really low level it may reach a point of no return no matter how much its environment improves. A strange, unproven idea but there may be something in it.

Whatever the reason, the polecat, though it disappeared from the whole of England and Scotland, survived in Wales. Today it flourishes not only in its old strongholds of Cardiganshire and south Merioneth but has spread even into the extremities: the Llŷn peninsula, the south-west of Pembrokeshire, north-east Wales and down the English border. It has even advanced east out of Wales, especially into Shropshire, Herefordshire and other counties.

So when you come to Wales can you expect to see polecats wherever you go? Far from it, for the polecat is rather a loner and is almost as nocturnal as a badger, much as it would like to be out by day, as occasionally it is. I have seen one in my garden, nosing its way into an outbuilding, obviously sniffing out rodents, and passing within six feet of me with outrageous carelessness. But normally polecats hide by day in the deepest cover. How then can I claim they are so common? Thank the traffic for that. Polecat corpses are now frequent enough on roads in many parts of Wales to assure us that they are present in good numbers, and often close to human habitation. Remember that 'polecat' in Norman times was 'poule-cat', the cat that played havoc with the pullets. He was a hanger round farms and cottages and so he still is, never happier than when he can hollow out a winter den in a haybarn.

But the polecat belongs to the wild as well—sea cliffs (but not islands), sand dunes, moorlands, peatbogs and all types of woodland, both broad-leaved and conifer. How many there are in the mountains nobody knows, but it is a fair guess that cliffs and block screes with their infinite hiding places are a refuge for polecats as well as the last remaining martens. The food of the polecat is varied, but its staple diet is the fieldmice, voles and young rabbits on which nearly all our flesh-eaters depend. And like most carnivores the polecat also takes frogs, beetles, worms, birds (it is not popular with poultrymen or owners of wildfowl collections) as well as enjoying various fruits in season.

Should you be lucky enough to meet with a full-grown polecat in daylight what you will see is a slender animal nearly two feet long, low-slung, short-legged, sharp-nosed, 'admirably formed', as the pioneer zoologist, Pennant, said in the eighteenth century, 'for insinuating itself into the smallest passages in search of prey'. Apart from a little white on its face it usually appears wholly black, but if it turns away from you, causing its dark outer hairs to separate, its thick underfur is seen to be mainly white. Caught in this position in your car's headlights it can surprise you by looking more white than black. In mid-Wales a red form used to be reported occasionally but I have seen only one red polecat in recent years.

It is not only at night that you may glimpse polecats from your car. But you are not likely to be as fortunate as a friend of mine last summer who saw not one but five polecats run in single file across a main road seven miles south-east of Aberystwyth in full sunlight. What better proof that polecats are not always solitary and nocturnal?

(1977)

'AMONG THE REAL WELSH'

GEORGE BORROW (1803-1881) IN WALES

Getting back to his hotel at Devil's Bridge after an exhilarating day on Plynlimon in 1854, George Borrow wrote: 'I walked along with a bounding and elastic step and never remember to have felt more happy and cheerful'. And why not? After all he was having a very long holiday, his health was excellent and so far the sun had shone more than it usually does in Wales. Yet, if we look into his previous few years, what do we find but a mood of bitterness and despair as he saw his literary reputation nosedive from the wild success of *The Bible in Spain* (1843) to the comparative failure of *Lavengro* (1851).

Why was he in such unexpectedly high spirits as he set off for Wales from his home in Norfolk at the end of July 1854? With a man of Borrow's odd temperament, who can ever say? Let us simply be thankful that the clouds of gloom had somehow unravelled themselves and that here he was gaily boarding a train at Norwich with his wife and teenage stepdaughter Henrietta, eager to be exploring west of Offa's Dyke. They came by way of Peterborough and Birmingham to Chester. After that their itinerary was complex. Sometimes they kept together, but more often Borrow went off alone and on foot. From Chester to Llangollen, for instance, while his wife and Henrietta took a train, Borrow walked the 20 miles so that he would get the full savour of his first venture across the border. He wanted Wales and Welsh speech to come gradually upon his senses.

Why did Wales and Welsh mean so much to one who had no obvious Welsh connections? There is the slender link that his father came from Cornwall and this may have made the boy curious about all things Celtic. What is certain is that, from an early age, he was fascinated by languages and that he eventually became proficient in a great many. Not that he studied Welsh merely to add another language to his collection. He was motivated by a keen desire to read Welsh poetry, and for a year, in his late teens, he took weekly lessons in spoken Welsh from a Welsh groom who had settled in Norwich.

So when, more than 30 years later, Borrow arrived in Wales (he had always been too busy to make the journey before), he was able to astonish the natives not only by speaking Welsh (however badly) but also by quoting their poets, even medieval ones. It was in these encounters with Welsh country folk that his sense of humour bubbled over. Everywhere he went he loved to see their mouths gape when this very tall, impressive and so obviously English gentleman addressed them in their own tongue. And address them he did incessantly, for above all it was people who interested him.

He was an incurable buttonholer of everyone he met along the road. Certainly his many chats (sometimes they became clashes) with local people are among the best things in *Wild Wales*. It is true, he usually showed himself coming out best in any argument, but this is all part of the fun. We can accept a few such eccentricities in an author as companionable as Borrow managed to be throughout *Wild Wales*.

One of his longings on this tour was to meet 'the real Welsh'. Of them he found few around Llangollen (where he spent most of his three and a half months in Wales). Llangollen was too near England, and most of its people were either bilingual or had no Welsh at all. It was not until he penetrated into the wild moorlands of Merioneth and came up the lonely valley from Llanuwchllyn to the pass of Bwlch-y-groes that he began to hear more and more people say *Dim Saesneg* (no English). 'S'sneg of no use here,' he was told to his delight. 'I was now indeed in

The Dee at Llangollen. During his long stay in Wales in 1854 George Borrow based himself mainly at Llangollen.

Wales among the real Welsh,' he rejoiced. He was lucky to have come when he did. Not so many years later, though he would have come upon individuals who were monoglot Welsh, it would have been nearly impossible to find a whole community to whom *S'sneg* was 'of no use'.

Another delight for him was to discover what a genuine culture flourished among the Welsh people, just the ordinary country folk he encountered everywhere, many of whom could discuss the old poetry and the complexities of Welsh metres and could tell him where the poets had lived and who their families were. Picture his pleasure in north Anglesey when he found not only the birthplace of Goronwy Owen but even a little girl who was a descendant of the poet and who wrote her name down for him in his notebook: *Ellen Jones yn perthyn o bell i gronow owen* (Ellen Jones belonging from afar to Goronwy Owen). When someone went to interview Ellen Jones half a century later she still vividly remembered her meeting with Borrow.

What are the best parts of *Wild Wales*? A matter of personal choice, certainly, but I prefer him when he is on the move on his own as on that trip into Anglesey. Even better is when he advances quickly south through mid-Wales. He goes swinging over the Berwyn moors and down to the lovely waterfall at Llanrhaeadr, where he 'never saw water falling more gracefully'; then through the wilds to Bala, Dinas Mawddwy and Machynlleth. From there he strides forcefully south over the hills, chancing upon an active lead-mine called the Welsh Potosi, where he is hospitably received and guided down to Ponterwyd. Here the inn at which he stayed now bears his name.

Where the Wye rises on Plynlimon. George Borrow drank at the source on November 5th, 1854.

George Borrow visited the churchyard of Strata Florida abbey in November, 1854, to see the yew tree under which the great medieval poet, Dafydd ap Gwilym, is reputedly buried.

His description of Plynlimon is one of the finest passages in the book—how in turn he drinks at the sources of Rheidol, Severn and Wye. Then he steps on next day to see Hafod Uchtryd, the house rebuilt by the scholarly Thomas Johnes after the dreadful fire of 1807, when nearly all his possessions, including irreplaceable literary treasures, had been lost. South again to the churchyard at Strata Florida, where he pays his respects to perhaps the greatest of all Welsh poets, Dafydd ap Gwilym, who (so tradition has it) is buried under a yew tree there.

After sleeping at Tregaron, the next morning he is soon at Llanddewibrefi, which launches him into the story of St David, who preached a famous sermon there; and so to Lampeter by midday. Little time to pause there as he goes triumphantly on over the southern hills and down to Pumsaint to sleep within sound of the River Cothi, a name which brings to his mind yet another beloved poet, Lewis Glyn Cothi. Next day he goes on to Llandovery: 'Feeling quite the reverse of tired, I chose the longest road, namely the one by Llanwrda, along which I sped at a great rate'.

Borrow takes kindly to Llandovery 'which I have no hesitation in saying is about the pleasantest little town in which I have halted in the course of my wanderings'. It is on a wild autumn day with violent winds tearing off the leaves in thousands that he leaves Llandovery and heads for the empty wastes of Black Mountain. Moorland mists engulf him and there are frightening precipices and darkness before he comes down to the comforts of an inn almost in Glamorgan, the tavern at Y Gwter Fawr, now called Brynaman.

He has now reached the end of wild Wales. Henceforth he is in the industrial south, walking onwards by way of Swansea, Neath, Merthyr Tydfil, Caerphilly and Newport. Finally, at Chepstow he drinks water from the mouth of the Wye in celebration of having drunk it at the source a short while before. He has supper at the best hotel, drinks port, sings Welsh songs, pays a hefty bill, buys a first-class ticket for the night train and is in London by four the next morning. So, in mid-November, his great Welsh walk ends as joyously as it had begun.

Borrow was an entertaining writer, a true open-air man (some even claim he was of gypsy descent) and a most joyful footslogger. Surely in our motorised age we should give due praise to one who thought nothing of walking 20 or 30 miles, not just once but day after day, through summer's heat and autumn's rains. But *Wild Wales*, when it appeared eight years later, was coolly received. It was a book which had to wait many years for its day to arrive, and now almost 120 years on, it has become a well-loved work and is still in the bookshops.

What has kept it going? Is it that its open-airness means so much more to us than it did to Borrow's contemporaries? The year Borrow came to Wales was also that of Thoreau's *Walden*, another book that in its day was a commercial failure, but which eventually won fame and became a tract for the open-air movement near the end of the century. As with *Walden*, so with *Wild Wales*: we can be sure there will always be readers for such fragrant and lyrical books.

(1981)

BIRDS OUTSIDE MY WINDOW

As I write at my table this morning I have distinguished company. Just outside the open door of my French window a great spotted woodpecker is hammering energetically at a cage of peanuts I have hung on a post. The bright sun gleams on his immaculate pied plumage and picks out a bright red bar across his nape—the mark of his sex. This woodpecker and I (he is easily known by his exceptional tameness) have been friends for months. He first came to our garden last July as one of a young family and was always the most approachable of the brood. Then a month later, when the rest of his tribe went away, he opted to stay and has been in or near the garden ever since.

One autumn day I had the whim to see if he was bold enough to come indoors. So I brought the nut cage into my room and hung it from a bookcase about 6 ft inside the open window. Then I sat back and waited. When he found the nuts had vanished from their post, he searched for them up and down the terrace, flying

When I brought a cage of peanuts indoors, a particularly bold great spotted woodpecker soon came in after them.

anxiously from perch to perch for several minutes. Then, clinging to a pole, he spotted them inside my room. He hesitated perhaps 30 seconds, then in he came to chip away at the nuts, though I was only a few feet distant. So life went on for the rest of the day—he was in and out frequently, readily accepting the sight of my pen moving back and forth across the page. And if I observed him furtively from under my brows he was still quite happy. But if I ever looked up suddenly, he was gone.

As I am not Henry Thoreau and do not live in a cabin by Walden Pond I did not really want my woodpecker to become a permanent lodger. So next day, though he might well have preferred his new indoor life (for there he had no rivals), I put the nut cage back on its post on the terrace where, instead of having it all to himself, he has to defend it against a whole bickering rabble of greedy nut-eaters. Not that his position at the top of the pecking order is ever seriously challenged, for all the smaller birds respect his long sharp bill. But the instant he flies away his place is usually taken by one of several nuthatches who share second place in the pecking league. Aggressive, quick as darts and very powerful for their size, they keep away most other birds but squabble endlessly with each other.

Every nuthatch has one incurable weakness: he is, above all things, a hoarder. He is never long at the nut cage before he yearns to take away a nut and hide it. So he works away at one until he can get it out through the mesh. For a moment he holds it in his beak as he works out his next move, and there is no mistaking the conflict in his mind: he hates to yield his position at the cage but he longs to fly away with his prize. And off he goes, usually to cache his nut in a wall at the back of the house, an act I often observe from the kitchen window.

His place at the nut cage is taken instantaneously either by a rival nuthatch or by a

Looking up the Nantcol valley in Meirionnydd to the pass of Ardudwy. Rhinog Fawr is on the left, Rhinog Fach on the right.

Cowslips on the Great Orme at Llandudno.

The spring squill is a familiar flower of the Great Orme.

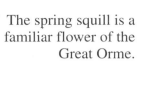

Hoary rockrose is a Great Orme speciality.

The middle reaches of the Wye are famous for their salmon.

A female chaffinch hoping for nut fragments to fall while the woodpecker is pecking at them.

greenfinch, for greenfinches, although not nearly as agile as nuthatches, are almost their equal in the pecking order. But very soon the first nuthatch comes darting back for another nut and away goes the greenfinch for a while. And so the skirmishing goes on for an hour or more while those other peanut enthusiasts, the tits and the siskins, flutter round in an agony of frustration without ever getting a look in. At such times even scavengers do better than tits or siskins. By scavengers I mean the chaffinches, robins, blackbirds, hedge sparrows and other less acrobatic birds which do not cling easily to feeders. Instead they wait patiently below and snap up fragments that come trickling down as woodpeckers and nuthatches peck wastefully at the nuts.

The woodpecker remains lord of the nut cage only until a grey squirrel comes rippling along. I suppose a squirrel, even a young one, looks too much like that dangerous carnivore, the stoat, for birds to take any chances with it. But squirrels eat so much and nuts are so expensive that I seldom feel like feeding them. So I frustrate them by greasing the pole on which the nut cage hangs. From the ground they can leap an amazing four feet, but the nut cage is higher than

that and they come sliding down again. Fortunately they are not very persistent. Half a dozen such failures are sufficient discouragement, and off they go in disgust.

A few feet from my nut cage I have a bird table. There the competition is much keener—a free-for-all that involves nearly every bird in the garden, including several bellicose blackbirds and irascible robins. (Mercifully our garden is quite free from starlings and house sparrows.) At the bird table, as at the nut cage, the squirrel is a tyrant who seems to get an unholy joy out of driving away his feathered rivals, especially the larger ones. But just occasionally a squirrel will be in a more comradely mood and, intent on his nibbling, will tolerate small birds on the table with him. Immediately below the squirrel in the pecking order is the jay, while my woodpecker friend, though so dominant at the nut cage, comes third. He will not go anywhere near a squirrel but he will stand and shriek defiance at the jay from only 12 inches distance, though a jay (I would have thought) is more dangerous than a squirrel.

My bird-table jay (always the same bird, I think) goes cautiously through life. Unlike the woodpecker, who often advises me of his approach with cries of *chick-chick*, the jay slips into the garden by stealth. Deep in my writing, I happen to glance up and there, perched watchful on the table, is the jay. For a minute or two he might be a stuffed bird, so rigid does he hold himself as he watches and listens. Then he relaxes and begins to feed, quite happy to gobble anything—corn, bread, cake, nuts, suet or meat. But, like the nuthatches, he loves to hoard. I note how his throat is beginning to distend with food and soon he flaps away over the hedge into the nearby pasture, where I can see him digging a hole in the turf to stow away his treasure. Does he remember where?

Sometimes I amuse myself by taking photographs of the birds as they feed. This is easy enough. All that is needed is to set up a camera on a tripod near the table or the feeder and then the shutter is operated by remote control from indoors. I nearly always use flashlight, for I have not the time to wait day after day for the sun to shine—a rather rare event in winter where I live, near the coast of Wales. At first I had fears that many of the birds would be scared by the crash of the shutter, but even the jay soon got used to it. (The flash is never noticed at all.) Another surprise was that my apparatus was accepted by all-comers without a moment's doubt. I had planned to camouflage it with foliage but, before I got round to doing so, I happened to look out of the window and there was the jay perched nonchalantly on my flash gun, gazing at the tempting spread on the table before him.

And what food we give the birds these days! It used to be kitchen scraps, but now we go out and buy on a lavish scale especially for them. Do we do it purely out of generosity? Or is it like paying for a television licence or buying a theatre ticket—a subscription for being entertained? Whatever the motive, it is certain that millions of birds are now being royally fed, and that millions of people get a great deal of joy out of watching them at it. I daresay that my writing output may suffer by my having a bird table outside my window. But what is this life if full of care . . .?

(1982)

A bird-table confrontation between a jay and a great spotted woodpecker.

IN SEARCH OF THE PICTURESQUE

1982, when this was written, marked the bicentenary of the book in which William Gilpin gave the world his thoughts on landscape painting. Their effect was long felt in artistic circles.

Thumb your way through old guidebooks and you will find that, even before the end of the eighteenth century, Ross was becoming popular as a launching-place for river tourism. The pioneer visitors to the Wye arrived there with grave intent. They came to look and look again at the beautiful stream, not for speeding seconds as their modern counterparts might do, but for days on end, days during which they were fully conscious of being the poets, painters and philosophers of a great new discovery—the art of looking at the British landscape.

This new vogue was largely the creation of the

Rev. William Gilpin (1724-1804), a native not of Ross or Monmouth or anywhere else around those parts but of far-off Cumberland, who had in 1782 published his *Observations on the River Wye*. It was in 1770 that he had first come to the Wye, fired with a missionary zeal for an artistic vision which he called 'the Picturesque', and which was to make him famous. But alas for the fate of some words: after Gilpin had launched it, 'Picturesque' was seized on by everyone who wrote a guidebook. It became the cliché of all clichés, and has remained limp and pallid ever since.

In this bicentenary year of Gilpin's classic of the Picturesque, it can do no harm to consider the impact of this word when it leapt into the language full of *brio*, meaning, excitement and inspiration. When it first set off down the Wye with William Gilpin, he carried it before him like

'Dr. Syntax in Search of the Picturesque' by Thomas Rowlandson. The drawing is a satire on Gilpin's ideas.

a banner which he hoped would attract converts from all directions. And so it did. From then on the Wye became a focal point for those who sought, to quote a contemporary guidebook, 'the picturesque, the pleasing, the tremendous and the sublime'. Among them it brought Wordsworth in 1798 to write his famous *Lines Composed a Few Miles above Tintern Abbey*.

Having proved his theory of the Picturesque to his own complete satisfaction down the Wye, Gilpin took it off in subsequent years on tour after tour in other parts of Great Britain. After each safari he came home to his study and worked up long essays on this matter so dear to his heart. After the Wye book he produced accounts of other sketching tours, thus creating what a critic rightly described as 'a new class of travels'.

Gilpin's Picturesque has long since become such an accepted way of looking at landscape that it is difficult for us to understand why it once caused so much excitement, and controversy too, when others besides Gilpin started their own theorising about the Picturesque. A verbose, tedious and inconclusive argument on the subject went on for years between Uvedale Price and Richard Payne Knight. Gilpin took no part in it: he had said his say and preferred to remain above the battle; so much so that, when someone asked him in 1795 what he thought of Price's definition of Picturesque, he replied: 'I am so little interested about the matter that I do not so much as know what his definition is, having never seen his book. If he explains the Picturesque better than I do, he is welcome'.

This comment seems typical of Gilpin, a man always very sure of himself. At the time of his Wye tour of 1770, he was, at 41, near the height of a successful career as headmaster of a preparatory school at Cheam, a school which he had transformed from mediocrity to being a model of enlightened education. He was, therefore, just the man to be laying down forthright rules about almost anything, including art, declaring that this scene was undoubtedly Beautiful, that one clearly Sublime (he was using Edmund Burke's terminology), yet neither scene was truly Picturesque (by which he meant simply that an artist could not easily compose it into a picture).

When he first came to Ross and was recommended to inspect the famous river view from the church, it was without hesitation that he gave it the thumbs-down: 'It consists of an easy sweep of the Wye; and of an extensive country beyond it. But it is not Picturesque. It is marked by no characteristic objects; it is broken into too many parts; and it is seen from too high a point'. In other words it was too wide a prospect to get onto a canvas, and there was nothing to lead the eye to some feature of central interest.

Downstream he came upon scenes more to his taste, especially where the valley narrowed and the topography was broken by cliffs and side dingles, or where there were steep, wild woodlands, jagged rocks or old buildings 'to give consequence to the scene'. His first truly artistic view came after four miles, when the ruins of Goodrich medieval castle appeared high above the water. 'This view, which is one of the grandest on the river, I shall not scruple to call *correctly Picturesque*.'

His further comments at Goodrich give us the essence of Gilpinism: 'Nature is always great in design but unequal in composition . . . Either the foreground or the background is disproportioned; or some awkward line runs across the piece; or a tree is ill-placed . . . or something or other is not exactly what it should be. She works on a vast scale . . . The artist in the meantime is confined to a *span*. He lays down his little rules therefore, which he calls the "principles of Picturesque beauty", merely to adapt such diminutive parts of nature's surfaces to his own eye, as come within its scope'.

So on he floated down the river, accepting this scene, rejecting the next, according to his 'little rules'. At Tintern he was severe on the abbey ruins as he saw them from a distance. In no way could they be composed in a Picturesque

Goodrich Castle. In his journey down the lower Wye in 1770, William Gilpin judged the view he got of this castle as 'correctly Picturesque'.

manner, for in those days they were 'encompassed with shabby houses'. It was only when he got in close that matters improved. Then he could take in the details, the wealth of green ivy against the grey stones, the colourful mosses, lichens and ferns, the 'penny-leaf and other humble plants', and find Tintern 'a very inchanting piece of ruin'.

His final Wye appraisal was at the Piercefield estate, now the site of the Chepstow racecourse. Here the river sweeps round its last superb bend, deep, brown and tidal beneath pallid limestone cliffs that are partly mantled by native trees. He loved it all: 'The winding of the precipice is the magical secret by which all these inchanting scenes are produced'. So he enthuses, but then, characteristically, lest we should get too carried away, he pulls us up short by adding: 'We cannot however call these views Picturesque'. Though, 'extremely romantic', they are too wide, they lack composition, they would not 'appear to advantage on a canvas'.

Though no great artist himself, Gilpin so managed to instruct others through his books that his influence can hardly be overstated. The British landscape was soon being depicted with universal enthusiasm, especially the wilder districts of the north and west. In search of fitting subjects, many an artist equipped himself with an oval mirror called a Claude glass. The viewer stood with his back to the landscape, moving the mirror until the ideal scene appeared in it as if framed in a picture. By this device many a view became Picturesque and was duly drawn or painted.

Often the drawing was deliberately and grossly inaccurate, for the artists were at liberty under the 'little rules' to introduce or remove castle ruins, clumps of trees or other parts of the landscape to meet the needs of the Picturesque. As Gilpin himself once put it: 'If nature gets wrong, I cannot help putting her right', an opinion which inevitably raised some hackles and long continued to do so. In America, for instance, many years after Gilpin's death, Henry

Thoreau, a champion of nature and distrustful of art, was totally contemptuous of Gilpin for seeing in nature nothing but pictures.

What would Gilpin think of the present scene, I wonder. I like to suppose that he would be almost wholly approving of this beautiful valley, which the modern age has touched comparatively lightly. He would surely be glad to see that we cherish the lower Wye valley as an Area of Outstanding Natural Beauty and the river as a Site of Special Scientific Interest. We have created nature reserves to safeguard the richer woodlands, as at Blackcliff and Wyndcliff, which are notable for wild and graceful yews, rare whitebeams, wild service trees, large-leaved and small-leaved limes and a ground flora that includes yellow bird's-nest, common wintergreen, wood cranesbill, Tintern spurge and several rare grasses and sedges.

Next time you go out to draw, paint, photograph or simply look at a beautiful natural scene, maybe you will spare a thought for the man who started us all off on this quest for 'that kind of beauty which would look well in a picture'. And should you visit the lower Wye you could hardly do better than have Gilpin's book with you (it was republished in 1973). If you can, take a boat in order to live his journey again and share the enthusiasms of this sensitive man who once wrote: 'If you have never navigated the Wye you have seen nothing'.

(1982)

The ruins of Tintern Abbey near which Wordsworth, attracted here by Gilpin's writings, wrote his 'Lines Composed a Few Miles above Tintern Abbey'.

A MUCH-CHERISHED RIVER

A treasure preserved in the Bodleian Library at Oxford is the Gough map of about 1360. It shows Wales grossly out of shape and quite dominated by a central mountain called 'Plimilemon', from which most of the country's rivers are radiating.

This totally false idea of Welsh geography seems to have persisted; for centuries afterwards writers were speaking of Plimilemon, Plinlimmon, Plynlimon (or in Welsh, Pumlumon) as the great mountain of Wales. Perhaps they were right. Perhaps to them Plimilemon was simply their term for what we call the Cambrian Mountains.

What we call Plynlimon today ranks far down the list of Welsh mountains in order of height. It must, however, always have had a romantic appeal because of its two cherished rivers, the Wye and the Severn, which rise so near to each other yet do not unite until the Wye has flowed for 156 miles and the Severn for 215 (vastly more if you include all the windings).

So Plynlimon is famous for its rivers. And though it is not the highest, it is certainly the spongiest of all the Welsh mountains, the one whose soils hold every drop of water they can for as long as they can, and so grow bog mosses, rushes and ankle-testing miles of molinia grass on a truly grand scale. 'A waste of russet-coloured hills' was George Borrow's description one autumn day. So it is for most of the year, and only for a brief summer do the tops green over.

The Wye and the Severn both spring from the eastern flank of the watershed, the slope that speeds them towards England. But while the Severn comes oozing out of a wide and squelchy peatbog, the Wye (two miles south-west) comes welling cleanly down a single gully to form a sparkling, yard-wide pool out of which the tiny stream goes splashing away through the moorlands, quickly gathering power. It gurgles round grey boulders and throws itself down slides and little falls, ever open to the broad light of day, not shadowed by conifers, as the juvenile Severn is for many miles.

Like all Welsh torrents near their source, the Wye is a starveling stream, cold, infertile, untouched by any minerals, hardly different from rainwater. Turn over its stones and you will find little in the way of animal life compared with further downstream. Its few plants are mostly

The source of the Wye at c. 2,000 feet on Plynlimon, Montgomeryshire.

liverworts, mosses and others that ask little of life. But last time I did find one plant of distinction—the starry saxifrage, here at the southern limit of its range—which does not seem to have been found along the Wye before. As with the flora, so with the birds. They are sparse indeed, even in summer: a few flitting pipits, a protesting wheatear, an occasional sandpiper, dipper, grey wagtail. In winter you will probably find no birds at all except a passing raven.

The Wye flows under its highest stone bridge at Pontrhydgaled, where it is crossed by the A44 (the Aberystwyth-Worcester road). Here, four miles from its source, it collects its first notable tributary, the Tarennig, and its lifestyle begins to change. Now it belongs less to the moors and ceases to be a beck dropping down rocks into deep green pools. Instead it escapes from its cleft to make musical meanders along miles of wide, flat, pebble washes. Here it becomes a salmon river in whose shallows great fish spawn in the short days of early winter. And here along the banks are the Wye's first broad-leaved trees— ash, alder, oak—and the highest woodland birds and insects.

At the ancient settlement of Llangurig the river has already dropped from 2,000 ft to 900 ft above the sea. But turning from east to south it still goes on in haste below farmhouses and hedgerowed fields down an ever-deepening valley that is almost a gorge where the Marteg stream comes hurrying in from the east under high steeps covered with rocks, bracken and heather. Trees now shadow the river ever more darkly, mosses hang thick and green on dripping rocks, and here at last are foodstores in the water to support a fair variety of small fishes— troutlets, minnows, bullheads, eels and brook lampreys.

By the time it reaches Newbridge and is half-way to the border, the river has changed again. The bare uplands of wild Wales are now far back up-country, and the river runs wide, strong yet calm through pastures where cattle increase with each mile and sheep get fewer. Here an Englishman can feel more at home for many of the place-names have not been in Welsh for centuries.

To put the change in purely river terms, the trout zone is here left behind and the world of the coarse fish is before you downstream. The Ithon, elegant tributary from the east, is home for many a grayling and silvery dace. And in Wye's deep pools are great chub, perch, pike and the alien barbel, all anathema to anglers who see these ever-increasing species as a threat to salmon and trout.

It is here around Builth that the salmon are still most numerous: among the river's noblest aboriginals, they are beautiful, healthful and strong after their ocean and river safaris. Were it not for angling, the Wye salmon might now be extinct, for there was a time, not so long ago, when the river was called 'an almost derelict fishery'. Only good management has restored it to prosperity. Curiously the salmon's close cousin, the sea-trout, which ascends some smaller Welsh rivers in legions, is scarcely reckoned a fish of the Wye at all.

At Builth Wells another delicious sidestream flows in—the Irfon. Rich in game fish, the Irfon has poured across igneous rocks along its way, and contains spa waters from Llanwrtyd and Llangammarch Wells. The Irfon has its special fishful tributary, the Chwefri, of which the ever knowledgeable Emilius Nicholson, who wrote the *Cambrian Traveller's Guide* of 1840, reported: 'The Chwefri is remarkable for the abundance of its trout which far exceed those of Wye or Irfon in firmness and flavour'.

Downstream from Builth, the river slips quickly between the acid moors of Epynt on the west and the lime-rich Aberedw Rocks of the unyielding eastern bank. Here its bed is the bare bones of the earth, potholed and chiselled into many strange shapes, bedrock that is scoured by racing water half the year. But in summer it is dry, and it is then the home of many plants that vanish in the floods of autumn. Of special interest here is the wild chives, a lime-seeking

Tufted saxifrage one of Britain's rarest alpines. It survives in Snowdonia mainly because it has been helped by plant-breeding experiments.

Looking south across the cliffs of Clogwyn y Garnedd, the botanically-rich east face of Snowdon.

Arctic saxifrage, a rarity in Snowdonia. Its flowers are reluctant to open fully.

The holly fern was almost exterminated in Snowdonia by the Victorian fern-collectors and is still very rare.

Alpine woodsia. In the whole of Snowdonia there are only two or three sites for this very rare and decreasing fern.

The Wye below Builth Wells. Wild chives grow in crevices of the riverside rocks, their purple-pink flowers showing from June to September.

plant that is extremely local in Britain but whose purple-pink flowers are conspicuous in June and July along miles of these riverside rocks and midstream islands. It anchors itself firmly against the snatch of fast water by worming its slim bulbs into crevices in the rocks.

Lime in the water also brings an increase in shelly animals. From here downstream molluscs increase greatly in numbers, and crayfish, so rare elsewhere in most of Wales, are abundant. This far upstream is about the normal limit of three elusive migratory fish: twaite shad, smelt and flounder. From here downstream waterside birds such as dipper and grey wagtail are probably commoner than anywhere else in Wales.

As it moves serenely down the middle of its wild floodplain, the Wye is already edged by the deep red soils it will flow through all across the rich lands of Herefordshire until it cuts its famous limestone gorge at Ross. At Monmouth it comes back to Wales and goes on down to the Severn estuary deep within the hills. But it is never a Welsh river again, only a margin to Wales, a beautiful selvedge of woodland, all the way to Chepstow.

Until this century many of the steeps above these last few miles of the Wye were under broad-leaved forest. Now there are miles, too many miles, of conifers. But there are patches of the old, semi-natural woodlands surviving here and there, and they are all a delight of different trees, shrubs, wildflowers, birds and insects. Amid oak and ash, beech and yew, there are three rare kinds of whitebeam, large-leaved and small-leaved limes and wild service. Spindle, dogwood, wayfaring tree and festoons of traveller's joy tell you how lime-rich the soil is. So does the wealth of common wildflowers— wood spurge, yellow archangel, wood melick and woodruff along with jungles of hart's-tongue and soft-shield ferns.

The nearer you get to Chepstow, the choicer becomes the flora, until at Black Cliff, then Wyndcliff (both are Forest Nature Reserves), the limestone cliffs, masked by scrub and woodland, tower high above main road and river with celebrated prospects of the winding Wye. Here you can botanise along rocky trails near the top of the crags; or descend countless steps to find shady, moist places amid a wilderness of trees and block scree, in a world green with mosses.

Bird's-nest orchid, lily-of-the-valley, common wintergreen, deadly nightshade, alternate-leaved golden saxifrage, narrow-leaved bittercress and narrow-leaved helleborine are just a few of the plants that people come miles to see. And there is the Tintern (or upright) spurge that belongs almost exclusively to these woods, a strange plant which, though usually hard to find, sometimes multiplies into large populations that show as yellow sheets on disturbed roadsides. Yet in a few years it retreats into obscurity.

In the long exploitation of the environment, ever since Neolithic times, human beings have kept few habitats in their primal state, and even moorland lakes and rivers which look so natural have probably not escaped some change. Maybe until the Bronze Age the banks of the upper Wye

The tidal part of the Wye near Piercefield, two miles north of Chepstow.

were deep in jungles of alder, hazel and oak right up to the river's source because that is the side of Plynlimon which enjoys shelter from Atlantic winds. Yet, though the forests have gone and the juvenile river in its present moorland setting is so impoverished, the water has at least kept its purity, though Plynlimon has a history of lead mining.

All down its course through Powys, the Wye remains clean and hospitable to life. True, there has been a most undesirable introduction of alien fish such as the barbel, and there could perhaps be others in the future, of robust species which are a threat to the survival of the most sensitive native fish. But generally the Wye remains in good heart, and quite rightly the whole river has been declared a Site of Special Scientific Interest, a status which should help to preserve it in its beauty and purity for ever.

(1983)

Narrow-leaved helleborine. This rare, decreasing orchid grows in woods in the lower Wye valley.

PLANTS IN HIGH PLACES

Although something like 14,000 years have slipped away since Britain said goodbye to its glaciers, even now we get our occasional severe winters to remind us that we are still living in the tail end of an ice age. What is more we still have true arctic or alpine plants growing on mountains as far south and west as those of Wales.

Not that these alpines are to be seen everywhere on our uplands. You can slog across mile after mile of ankle-punishing country and see nothing more exciting than bilberry, crowberry, sheep's fescue and mat grass. But you may get your reward at last when you have crossed the botanical deserts and reached one of those ice-carved mountain hollows called corries or cirques. Only then can you hope to see the arctic-alpine vegetation at its happiest.

But what is happiness for most of our native alpines? It is to be growing on a crag that is precipitous enough to defeat all sheep and goats;

a crag that faces north or east to escape the drying effects of sun and prevailing winds; a crag with many ledges, fissures and caverns where water drips and oozes perpetually out of soft and rotten lime-rich rocks that break down quickly into nutritious soils.

Such cliffs can be spotted from afar by their greenness. And when you get to them you can look up and up and see how, for hundreds of feet, they are thickly upholstered with plants of many kinds, the most abundant alpines being starry saxifrage, purple saxifrage, roseroot, moss campion, alpine scurvy-grass, alpine meadow rue, mountain sorrel and a few others.

This community of Snowdon alpines (plus a handful of rarities) has a unique position in the world. It is not only very close to the mild Atlantic, but its altitude too (mostly 1,500-2,500 ft) is quite unalpine. Yet here we find the alpine saxifrage (*Saxifraga nivalis*), a plant that

Arctic chickweed, a rare plant of Snowdonia.

124

feels at home at over 6,000 ft as far north as Norway, and flourishes also at nearly 14,000 ft in the Rockies. Not that it can really be said to flourish in Snowdonia. Indeed it only just holds on, and is a considerable rarity.

Another rarity is *Lloydia serotina*, which we parochially call the Snowdon lily, but which happens to be the most widespread lily in the world, though marvellously discontinuous in its range. Outside Snowdonia it grows in the Alps, the Carpathians, the Himalayas, arctic Russia and other isolated places in Eurasia. And on the opposite side of the northern hemisphere, it is found very high in the Rockies.

At many of its stations it is reported to be either infrequent or rare. In Snowdonia, where it grows on half a dozen lime-rich cliffs spread over about seven miles from east to west, this tiny, white lily has the distinction of being the only bulbous plant in the alpine community. The Snowdon lily's huge but greatly interrupted world range has led to the assumption that in the cold conditions immediately after the ice age its distribution was continuous all across the lowlands of the northern hemisphere, but that, like other present-day alpines, it retreated to the mountains as the climate became temperate. However, why it survived in Wales, yet not elsewhere in Britain, especially Scotland, still awaits an explanation.

Compared with that of Switzerland, the alpine flora of Snowdonia is scanty indeed, but its very meagreness makes it all the more interesting. For here we have a small community of alpines growing in such mild conditions that they have to share their living space with many lowland species, chiefly plants of woodland origin which crept into the uplands as the broad-leaved forests reached their maximum altitude about 5,000 years ago.

The forests went long ago, and have been prevented from returning by grazing animals, but the wildflowers have persisted on inaccessible ledges, where they enjoy woodland-like conditions of coolness, dampness and fertility.

So up there in spring the lovely alpines bloom amid a fine show of primroses, wood anemones, early purple orchids, moschatel, bugle, wood sorrel and other woodlanders. And as the months go by, the lowlanders get ever more assertive, with tall stands of valerian, angelica, globe flower, hawkweeds, devil's-bit scabious, water avens and a crowd of other hustlers which the alpines of high mountains abroad do not have to contend with.

A further peculiarity about some of Snowdonia's alpines is that they so clearly depend on the presence of lime in the soil, yet in the Alps and elsewhere these same species flourish on quite limeless rocks. Alpine saxifrage, Snowdon lily and alpine meadow rue are examples.

Why this remarkable difference between their Snowdonian lifestyle and the one they enjoy in the Alps? Is it that, in the rather unfavourable circumstances under which they struggle to survive in Wales, these plants need some extra comfort which lime provides? Perhaps it helps them to take up phosphates or other chemicals without which they can manage in the more suitable climate of the Alps.

When are the alpine flowers at their best? It is a matter of choice. Some might say there is nothing to be compared with the splashes of vivid colour that the purple saxifrage brings to the ledges in March and April, when the vegetation all round is still in its winter sleep. After that there is a long gap until late May and early June, when the cushions of the moss campion turn bright-pink with flowers, the roseroot opens yellow and there is pure whiteness from starry saxifrage, mossy saxifrage and alpine scurvy-grass.

Sea pink, a strange intruder from the coast, also begins to flower then. So do some of the rarer species like Snowdon lily, whose time is very short; mountain avens, which is extremely rare in Wales; arctic chickweed, whose white flowers are large for the size of the plant; twisted whitlow grass, so called because of the shape of its seedpods; alpine cinquefoil, if you are lucky enough to find this yellow-flowered beauty, and black alpine sedge (*Carex atrata*), so distinctive with its large, dark heads.

By mid-July the best of the show is over, but there are still a few treasures to be sought. The alpine saxifrage is one of these later flowerers. So is another rarity, the alpine bistort. Among the last comes the alpine saw-wort, whose purple spikes you may see in early September along with the delicate white flowers of grass of Parnassus, which looks even more elegant on a mountain ledge than it does in the wet meadows of the lowlands.

If we care to speculate about the past, can we assume that there were more species of alpines in Wales in the tundra period between the end of the ice age and the coming of the Atlantic-type climate? If so, then the Snowdon alpines take on a rather funereal look as a community doomed to extinction as the ice age recedes ever further into history. Or should we take the view that, despite temporary fluctuations, our weather has not seriously changed for centuries and that our alpines are not really under any climatic threat?

They are, after all, the same species which the pioneer botanists found here in the seventeenth century. The only loss in recent times has been the Irish saxifrage (*S. rosacea*), if indeed it is completely extinct. And there has been a near loss in the tufted saxifrage (*S. caespitosa*), which is currently being helped by raising its seeds elsewhere and returning the seedlings to Snowdonia. Though there may have been few natural changes over the past 300 years or more, there have been serious losses caused by the depredations of botanists and gardeners, who have played havoc with the rarer ferns and also with the Snowdon lily, whose bulbs are easily removed from the shallow soils which cover them.

A curious episode in the history of Snowdon's alpines came in the 1920s when a group of enthusiasts leased some land in one of Snowdon's corries, where they broadcast the seeds of several kinds of Asiatic alpines in the hope of creating a flowery mountain garden like the famous one at Floraire, near Geneva. It was an exercise which brought sharp comments from those who feared that these foreign plants might be a threat to the native flora.

The experiment, persisted in for several years, eventually inspired a light-hearted leading article in *The Times* of October 22, 1932, which commented: 'Enthusiastic amateurs may have seen radiant visions of a summer sea of gentians, fritillaries, primroses and other exotic beauties which naturalists have discovered of recent years in China and Tibet. Snowdon would have none of it. She proved a very stepmother to the little strangers. She called on the Atlantic to drench them in salt tears; she encouraged the hardy children of her own slopes and screes to smother them; and she led her sheep to browse on them and her hordes of slugs to devour them. And she did it all so thoroughly that now there scarcely remains a trace of the bravely but vainly planned experiment'.

Next day's *Times* had a letter from the president of the Linnean Society 'deprecating most strongly' this experiment, and suggesting that if any money were to be spent on Snowdon it ought to go towards the conservation of the native flora. In the event, about 40 years were to pass before Snowdon became a National Nature Reserve, thus opening a promising new phase in the fortunes of its alpine flora.

(1983)

CAMERA-SHY RAVENS

Photographing ravens is easy, a friend told me. All you have to do is put meat out for them every day in front of a hide, and soon they will be coming down like sparrows. This was an attractive idea because, although I had had the pleasure of living with ravens as neighbours over many years, I had never managed to get close enough to photograph them. After centuries of persecution they have learned to be the wariest of birds.

I decided to do what my friend recommended. I set up a hide within my garden fence, arranged for a supply of offal and put down my bait on the sheep pasture outside my garden. The date was October 28, and I reckoned the operation might take a couple of weeks if I could give it about two hours a day.

As so often in nature photography, things did not go to plan. This was not from any shortage of ravens, for there were over 50 of them roosting in the nearby wood every night. The trouble was that just then they were not at all meat-minded. Instead they were frolicking all day in the tree-tops, gobbling up an abundant harvest of acorns. For the first two weeks nothing came to my bait except a mass of bluebottle flies.

By mid-November the acorns had all gone—eaten or hidden away by an army of birds and mammals—and at last my meat began to attract the attention of crows and magpies. Hoping the ravens would come to join the feast, I decided to carry on with the baiting, though the time I had allotted for the project had expired. It was of no avail. Day after day I kept my vigil in the hide, and day after day ravens passed croaking overhead without showing any interest in the spread I had laid before them. What had started as an allegedly easy task now began to take the form of a challenge.

Then, on December 10, it looked as if my luck might change. The weather had suddenly turned cold, a thin layer of snow covered the fields, and

I spent my days in a hide in the snowy winter of 1981-2 before I eventually got this photograph of a raven on the remains of a dead sheep.

as I crept into the hide I could hear excited raven voices very close. The noise was coming from two ravens stabbing their powerful beaks into a sheep which had died that morning on the other side of the pasture. The situation looked promising. I dragged this sheep in front of my hide and waited. And I went on waiting for a frustrating couple of hours while the two ravens circled over, or perched in the nearby trees, but would not come down. Clearly they distrusted my hide, though I had taken the precaution of covering it with branches.

The cold persisted, and by December 18 the fields were really deep in frozen snow. By now all birds were hungry and up to 40 bold and quarrelsome crows were feeding and fighting at my dead sheep throughout the day. More snow fell, and I had to clear it off my bait every morning so that the birds could find the meat. Then, two days before Christmas, the first buzzard arrived. It landed by the sheep, which was now rather skeletal, stepped calmly among the scrum of crows and began to tear at the meat. The crows all stood well back in a respectful but agitated circle. They were clearly seething with frustration, and every now and then one of them sneaked up behind the buzzard and tweaked its tail. These attacks the buzzard never seemed to notice.

This proved to be an exciting day. As soon as the buzzard had flown away, the crows were violently scattered by a red kite that suddenly swooped among them, snatched a piece of offal, and was gone. The action was so swift that only a ciné-camera could have caught it. This kite, though hungry, was extremely nervous. It came back in a few minutes and made another lightning grab at a piece of meat, but all I captured on my negative was a blur. I never saw that beautiful but timid kite again.

The weather eased over Christmas, but in January it turned cold again. More snow fell, days were gloomy and there was not enough light for photography. All the same, I put on extra socks and pullovers and dug through the snow to my hide just to see what the birds were up to. My meat restaurant was now well known among the local crows and buzzards. Jays showed a mild interest, but clearly they are not much given to meat-eating. A few magpies came, but like most country magpies, as distinct from urbanised magpies, they were always very shy. Even chaffinches, robins, great tits and blue tits were finding something to eat on the now very scanty remains of my dead sheep.

Of all my visitors it was the buzzards that I most enjoyed watching. As the days went by, they became ever more bold. Sometimes they saw me enter the hide, yet never paused in their feeding. I have no idea how many different buzzards I entertained: they were usually careful to come one at a time to avoid conflict. On the only occasion that two came together they went for each other with murderous intent, tumbling wildly all over the ground until one of them retreated. If left alone, the buzzards would feed steadily for about half an hour, sometimes gulping down massive chunks of meat. They ignored the crash of my camera shutter, which made the crows leap a foot off the ground although they had heard it scores of times.

One day a large female buzzard so over-indulged herself with all this good food that she could hardly move, reminding me of those vultures on the plains of Africa that get so bloated with carrion they cannot walk. This overloaded buzzard stood a long while and then decided to fly away. She managed to get airborne, but when she tried to reach the lowest bough of an oak she missed it and crash-landed in the snow. She was still standing there when I left the hide an hour later.

Another fortnight passed amid snow and icy winds, and still no ravens came. By now their absence was less surprising because sheep were dying every day and carrion eaters had a wide choice of restaurants. I suspected that the crows and ravens, disliking each other's company, had worked out an agreement whereby the crows had their private dead sheep and the ravens had theirs. By misfortune the dead sheep in front of my hide must have been apportioned to the crows.

My feeling of frustration was increased by a phone call from my photographic friend who reported that he was having a marvellous time in his hide a few miles away. He was taking pictures of kites, and his only trouble was too many ravens. He was having to drive them off because they were keeping the kites away from the bait.

The time came when I had to go away from home and abandon my project. But the weather, still cold, was now sunny, and I decided to have one last session in the hide. By chance that was the day when a raven at last broke with convention and came to inspect my dead sheep. He did not stay long. Maybe he did not fancy the menu. More likely he objected to all those snarling crows. He beaked into the carcass without enthusiasm and then flew quietly away. But I got my picture.

(1984)

128

SNOWDONIA FOR FERNS

'As stiff and prickly as a spike of little holly leaves.' So in 1840 in his *History of British Ferns* Edward Newman described a species whose identity he was not quite sure about, those being early days in the study of some of our rarer ferns. He called it the 'Alpine Prickly Fern' but the name did not catch on and in his next book four years later the name he used was 'Holly Fern', as we still call it today.

Writing of his beloved ferns Newman can hardly have dreamt that his books were going to play a major part in sparking off a revolution in taste. Yet very soon the Victorian fern craze (or 'pteridomania') was in full swing and ransacking the countryside for ferns had become a fashionable pastime. A considerable trading in ferns also developed and soon even on the summit of Snowdon you could buy roots of holly fern for sixpence from local men who risked their lives climbing the crags in search of this and other rarities.

Fern collecting long remained an extraordinary obsession. Though it was at its height in the middle third of the nineteenth century, books were still being published in the early years of the twentieth advising their readers how and where to obtain ferns from the wild. Some people dried them and kept them in albums. Others pressed them for use as house decorations. At first any large and beautiful frond served this purpose. But the emphasis soon shifted to an interest in unusual varieties.

This new pursuit was taken very seriously and every freak or sport was solemnly given a ponderous Latin name. Some authors catalogued as many as three hundred varieties of the common lady fern, over seventy of the male fern and over sixty of the broad buckler fern. One nurseryman had eight hundred varieties on his fern list.

All this collecting of fronds was vandalistic enough but far worse was the uprooting of whole plants for growing in gardens and indoors. And the trouble got really serious when the rarer species began to be pillaged. Writers of books and articles urged their readers to make sure they were properly equipped for the hard work of digging ferns out of rocky places, a typical armoury for the occasion being 'a small garden fork, a stout chisel, a hammer, a strong knife, a trowel, a covered basket and a spade'.

One thing all fern collectors soon realised was that most species prefer a cool damp climate and are therefore in their greatest profusion in the north and west of Britain. Rain-washed Snowdonia, rich in ferns and easily reached from south-east England and the Midlands, especially when the railways developed, became a favourite hunting ground where, from the sea cliffs to the mountain tops, many exciting finds were made.

It was usually where the sea winds blow that the seekers found a charming little evergreen called lanceolate spleenwort growing on rocks and walls. And even more full of ocean-longing is the sea spleenwort which grows only on cliffs or in caves that are kept ever moist and cool by frequent bathing in salt sea spray.

Inland the pteridopterists loved to explore the wooded vales, the fairy glens and shadowy gorges richly upholstered with lady ferns, buckler ferns and other abundant woodlanders. High on the branches of even the tallest oaks they saw thickets of polypody ferns waving to them like the epiphytic plants of tropical rain forests. On wet streamside rocks they found a drapery of the moss-like Wilson's filmy fern that is still not uncommon in Snowdonia; and occasionally the much scarcer Tunbridge filmy fern which, despite its name, is extremely rare in eastern England.

At a very few sites, especially where waterfalls thundered and splashed, there was (and happily still is) the elegant hay-scented buckler, a fairly large fern which C. Johnson in his *Ferns*

Green spleenwort is locally abundant in Snowdonia but only where the rocks are lime-rich.

of Great Britain (1855) thought might be 'a wanderer from the Azores', so emphatically western and south-western is it in Britain. But the great prize of damp streamside rocks and cool caves was the Killarney fern which, alas, is now almost extinct in Snowdonia. It would be sad indeed to lose it altogether because elsewhere in the world this tender fern is largely tropical and it is wonderful to find it as part of the native British flora.

A truly rare little fern is the unmistakable forked spleenwort whose narrow leaves divide at the end like the tongue of a serpent. It prefers acid rocks and limeless soil and has a special liking for the vicinity of lead-mines. In the bad old days this distinctive fern, always rare, was very seriously depleted. But in the more conservation-minded times in which we live we have learnt to enjoy our ferns without molesting them.

There are two mountain ferns that are widespread and abundant: the beech fern, easily known by its lowest pair of leaves—they hang like a drooping moustache; and the lemon-scented fern, a large plant which crowds the banks of upland streams, its fronds often curving elegantly over the water. And there is that special delight, the oak fern, a species of strange ecology: you can go for many miles across the hills and see no sign of it then suddenly there it is, not just a plant or two but a whole scree carpeted with its beautiful, delicate fronds.

The more lime there is in the rocks the more likely we are to find the graceful brittle bladder fern which, though it grows here and there in the lowlands, is vastly more abundant in the mountain cliffs. But no fern more emphatically announces the presence of calcium than the bladder fern's frequent companion, the green spleenwort, which is much like the maidenhair spleenwort so common on walls in the lowlands. Green spleenwort, readily known by the greenness of its midrib, is a fern to give us a thrill of anticipation because its message is that we have reached the special rocks where we are sure to find a wealth of other alpines, not only ferns but flowering plants as well.

So we come to that elite trio of ferns: the holly fern and the two kinds of woodsia. To be sure of seeing holly fern you had better go to Scotland where locally it is abundant and reasonably accessible. But to find it in Snowdonia you need a great deal of luck or help and to be prepared for some energetic scrambling up slippery wet rocks. Holly fern is a most attractive plant— robust, tough, leathery and with pronounced saw-like edges to its leaves. On average these are six or eight inches long but in deep fertile crevices they can grow much bigger.

In comparison the two woodsias are distinctly dwarfish, especially in Snowdonia. The smaller one, the alpine woodsia, has a struggle to reach an inch and a half; the larger, the oblong woodsia, makes a little over two inches if it is doing well. In the whole of Snowdonia there are only two or three known sites for the woodsias and at each spot the number of plants is very small. Their first discoverer, the eminent Welsh botanist Edward Lhuyd, described them three hundred years ago as 'Very rare even at Snowdon' and the nineteenth-century collectors left them still closer to the edge of extinction.

Common or uncommon, nearly all these alpine ferns grow most profusely in the great corries which time and erosion have gouged out of the flanks of the mountains. But if we go up to the exposed summits high above the corries, what ferns shall we find? To answer that question we don't need to be great mountaineers. We can get on the Snowdon train at Llanberis. Through the carriage windows, as the engine thumps us steeply upwards, we see first the luxurious ferns of the oakwoods; after that we climb up through the bracken zone which mercifully does not last long because this all-smothering fern has no love of frost. Then, up in the zone of coldness, we begin to see the alpines and we discover that the one which goes with us all the way to the summit is an abundant species of acid screes and rocks, the parsley fern, of which W. J. Hooker wrote in 1861: 'This elegant fern is so totally unknown in all the south and middle of England that botanists who visit the north-west are struck by its great beauty'.

What will the future bring to the fortunes of these mountain ferns? Snowdonia is too far from the Arctic, too near the Atlantic and too lacking in altitude to be really good country for alpines. Its summers are too cool and damp, its winters an uncomfortable mixture of mildness and severity. Not only its rare ferns but also several of its flowering plants are near to total obliteration and maybe it only needs an extra dose of atmospheric pollution to tip the balance against them. More optimistically we can cite the case of the tufted saxifrage. This declining species, which had been reduced in Snowdonia to a mere two or three plants, has been successfully reintroduced in its native habitat after cultivating it and multiplying it in a nursery. So perhaps the same will be done for the holly and Killarney ferns and those endearing little woodsias?

(1987)

131

INDEX